# THE ART OF COARSE DRINKING

3⁰⁰ M
K9

Also in Arrow by Michael Green

*Michael Green*

# THE ART OF COARSE DRINKING

*Illustrated by John Jenson*

*What mortals make the sky look bluer?*
*I know a few and one's the Brewer*
ANONYMOUS VERSE IN SALOON-BAR

ARROW BOOKS

ARROW BOOKS LTD

*3 Fitzroy Square, London W1*

An Imprint of the Hutchinson Publishing Group

London Melbourne Sydney Auckland
Wellington Johannesburg Cape Town
and agencies throughout the world

First published by
Hutchinson & Co (*Publishers*) Ltd 1973
Arrow edition 1975

*This book is published at a net price and
supplied subject to the Publishers Association
Standard Condition of Sale registered under
the Restrictive Trade Practices Act 1956*

© Michael Green 1973
illustrations © Hutchinson and Co (*Publishers*) Ltd

*Made and printed in Great Britain by
Hunt Barnard Printing Ltd, Aylesbury, Bucks*

ISBN 0 09 909960 8

Dedicated to the Marquis of Granby

*The man who inspired ten thousand pubs*
*without anybody having the faintest idea*
*who the hell he was.*

# Contents

# Author's Note

Since I once received an angry letter from a reader who ruptured himself while trying to perform one of the strokes described in *The Art of Coarse Golf*, I should like to issue the following warning: The Author takes no responsibility for any damage caused through being taken too seriously.

*Michael Green*

# 1 An Introduction to Coarse Drinking

*And may there be no moaning of the bar . . .*

TENNYSON

Alcohol is a peculiar way of achieving happiness. To start with, it's basically nauseating and a taste for it in various forms such as beer and whisky has to be acquired. Technically it is a poison and leaves bad after-effects; and it is habit-forming. Altogether it would be far more convenient if Nature had provided a substitute which produced only pleasant results such as gaiety and never hideous things like Boozer's Gloom. And which came in a more convenient form for distribution, such as a bean. One of the difficulties about drink is that it is difficult to carry it around, involving as it does clumsy cans and bottles.

Drink is also associated with ill-health. The drunkard of the novel is rarely a man of iron constitution. Many regard the public-house as a sort of do-it-yourself destruction headquarters, where the customers poison themselves with alcohol, ruin their lungs with tobacco and spoil their digestions with crisps.

Yet drink survives and needs no apology from me, when the majority of the human race, including many of its wisest members, have been defending it for thousands of years. In youth it offers stimulus, in old age comfort. And as regards its ill-effects, my old Uncle Walter always says, "Remember, my boy, that more people die from drowning each year at Land's End, than die from alcohol at Land's End."

While admitting that Uncle Walter's logic is slightly distorted, it is doubtful if alcohol has contributed more to human misery than, for instance, the internal combustion engine. It is equally doubtful if a bottle of beer does any more harm than a bottle of lemonade, although five bottles might.

As regards Coarse Drinking, I think the best way of explaining it is to tell a story about my curious friend Askew. Askew celebrated his 22nd wedding anniversary by toasting his wife with a single measure of gin for every year of his married life. There are 36 singles in a bottle. As a result of this foolish feat, he first of all tried to climb the tree in the back garden, and fell off at the lowest branch. He was soon, however, reduced to coffee and aspirin and when I left he was clutching his stomach and vowing that if he recovered he would be good and kind to people for the rest of his life, which wouldn't be long.

Next day he rang me up.

"How do you feel after last night?" he asked anxiously.

I said I felt quite well, considering everything.

"Well I wanted to warn you," said Askew. "I felt absolutely awful this morning. Never had a hangover like it. *Obviously there must have been something wrong with the tonic waters to give me a headache like this.* I've thrown the rest away. Bad tonic water is poison, old man."

I have put the key sentence in italics. For there you have the spirit of Coarse Drinking. A Coarse Drinker is a man who blames his hangover on the tonic and not the gin.

He will be most reluctant to admit that alcohol made him ill. He'll blame the bitter lemon, the water he put in his whisky, even the cherry in his cocktail. My old Uncle Walter would invent the most outrageous excuses for hangovers. When struck by a particularly bad one he excused himself to my Aunt Gladys by saying, "Mother, I feel terrible, I believe I must have caught a germ off a dirty glass last night."

Why should a Coarse Drinker behave in this peculiar way? I think it is because alcohol is important to him (or her). This doesn't mean he is a drunk. He can be a

*He'll blame the bitter lemon, the water he put in his whisky, even the cherry in his cocktail*

half-pint-a-day sipper. But he has a genuine affection for the stuff and appreciates its importance as a social lubricant in the artificial life we lead.

A Course Drinker is not likely, when friends call, to keep them hanging about for an hour and then say, "Oh, I'm forgetting, perhaps you'd all like a drink?" Neither does he need some coy excuse for a drink, such as having one for the road, or because it's a hot day. He needs a drink because he needs a drink.

He is not one to be deceived by hypocrisy and pre-conceptions. In drinking, as with all Coarse activities, it is necessary, as Dr. Johnson said, "to clear the mind of cant." In *The Art of Coarse Sailing* I described a Coarse Sailor as one who, in a crisis, forgets all the phoney nautical language and shouts, "For God's sake, turn left!" The Coarse Drinking equivalent would be if four old friends arrived and there was nothing in the house to drink except cooking wine. Some people would apologise that there wasn't anything to drink. The Coarse Drinker would offer the cooking wine and if the guests were Coarse Drinkers they'd drink it and tell him how awful it tasted while asking for more.

One way of telling a Coarse Drinker is when he is eating out. Your true Coarse Drinker looks at the wine list first, chooses the booze, and then picks the food to go with it. This always leads to trouble with Uncle Walter in restaurants, because a lot of waiters have a habit of handing out the menu and then vanishing without leaving the wine list.

"My dear fellow," says Uncle Walter impatiently, "how *can* I tell you what I want to eat until I have chosen the drink?"

Indeed, the service of drink in restaurants leaves much to be desired for Coarse Drinkers. For instance, if you like a glass of white wine served on its own before the meal (as I do) it is impossible to get it without the first course as well. White wine ordered with a separate fish course invariably arrives with the steak; and if you order an extra bottle of red to go with the cheese it usually arrives just as you're putting on your hat and coat. Beer is all too often rationed to one glass.

At Uncle Walter's wedding anniversary a bottle of red wine ordered to go with the cheese arrived with the bill. "What's this?" commented Walter sourly. "A nightcap?"

Perhaps I may quote another incident involving the Dreaded Askew as an example of the Coarse Drinker's attitude to drink, and indeed to life itself.

In his bachelor days it was Askew's habit to drink a bottle of white-shield Worthington pale ale every morning in bed as soon as he woke up (yes, I too, find it revolting, but apparently he didn't). He claimed that it toned up the system, stimulated the bowels, invigorated the mind and gave him courage to face another day.

In due course he got married. On the morning after the wedding, his bride was rather surprised when he got up and left the hotel bedroom. For a moment she imagined he might have gone to pick her an early morning rose, still wet with dew, but Askew merely returned holding a bottle of Worthington which he poured into a toothbrush glass and drank.

"It was," says Askew, "our first quarrel. Not bad, to have it only 16 hours after the wedding." Although it is only fair to say that Mrs Askew's version is different. She claims the quarrel arose from the fact that when she snuggled up to him in bed and said affectionately, "Darling, do you think we shall have a baby?" Askew replied, "I hope so, I don't want this bloody performance every night."

Many famous men appear to have been Coarse Drinkers. A particularly fine one (before he was compelled to give up drink for health reasons) was Dr. Samuel Johnson and I always cherish his remark that "he who does not mind his belly, will hardly mind anything else." Dear, gentle Jane Austen may have been one as well. She once wrote in a letter to a friend, "I find many Douceurs in being a sort of

*Dear, gentle Jane Austen may have been one as well*

Chaperon for I am put on the Sofa near the Fire and can drink as much wine as I like . . ."

A Coarse Drinker is in good company. He need not be ashamed of the priority he gives to drink.

### A COARSE DRINKING QUIZ

A bane of the drinker's life is these wretched pseudo-psychological tests in magazines and newspapers. Whenever the subject is drink I always score maximum points and according to the quiz this means I am an alcoholic. I refer to questions like: Do you wake up at 3 a.m. desperate for a drink? Do you drink between meals? Have you ever had a day without alcohol? Are you miserable until you have a drink? (The answers to those questions being, in my case, Yes, Yes, No, Yes.)

So it is with some diffidence that I submit yet another quiz on the subject. However, readers might like to discover whether they themselves are Coarse Drinkers, or how far down the slippery slope they have descended. So for their benefit, I have compiled the following quiz:

1. Do you know the difference in licensing hours between Gloucester and Sheringham during the summer?

2. Have you ever entered a restaurant, had a drink at the bar, and finished up by not eating?

3. Have you ever tried to save money by cutting down on dry ginger, bitter lemon, tonics and lemonade rather than alcohol?

4. Have you ever tried to save weight by reducing your intake of soft drinks?

5. Would you shudder if offered a glass of Coco-Cola without rum?

6. Have you ever tried to persuade someone to serve you drink after licensed hours?

7. Are you afraid to keep spirits in the house because you sit in front of the television and drink them all?

8. Do you feed beer to your dog?

9. After a party, have you ever sneaked round all the half-empty glasses and finished them off?

# 2 The Good Old English Pub

*"Ah, more than school or church or hall*
*The village inn's the heart of all."*
*So spake the brewers' P.R.O.*
*A man who really ought to know*
*For he is paid for saying so.*

JOHN BETJEMAN

Pubs are like beds. People spend a surprisingly large percentage of their lives in them, yet take them for granted. If a man spends two hours a day (which is not long if lunchtime is included), six days a week, inside a pub he will have something like 7% of his adult life there. Many people are there a lot more, of course. Since a Coarse Drinker will almost certainly spend a fairly large proportion of his life in pubs he must never take them for granted. He must sometimes stop to think about the subject and learn to cut through the tangle of myth and hypocrisy which surrounds it.

People are always referring to the traditional English pub, but nobody seems quite sure what it is. Probably, if pressed, most people would admit to a vague idea of something old and quaint, preferably with horse-brasses and beams, selling traditional food and possibly "olde" type drinks such as mead and beetroot wine. Not to mention the genial, beaming mine-host behind the bar.

Unfortunately, although there are plenty of places like this, they are these days rarely traditional, typical or unspoilt. They have probably been renovated at enormous expense, perhaps with plastic beams and are being run by a vast, international brewing concern.

We are conditioned to erect an image of the traditional English pub (often by the advertising of the very people who are destroying it). But the genuine olde Englishe pub

10. Is capital punishment justified in the case of a per who fails to buy his round?

11. Have you ever finished your drink even though y have a nasty suspicion something unpleasant is floating it?

*Score ratings:*

Eleven Yesses: You are not merely a Coarse Drinker you're in danger of becoming an alcoholic. But then, all quizzes produce that result.

Seven Yesses: Fairly Coarse. Probably better as a boozer than a husband.

Five Yesses: Needs to try harder.

Three Yesses: You are in danger of becoming a prig. •

No Yesses: Sir, I don't wish to know you.

with its beams and horse brasses is these days not so much an olde Englishe pub as an olde Englishe investment and its owners treat it as such. That usually means evicting the old couple who used to run it; pulling down the cottage next door to make a car-park; turning the public-bar into an expensive restaurant serving Italian food; putting a disco in the old barn; and, of course, discouraging those stupid pensioners and locals whose custom brought little profit. In other words, turning the place into everything the olde Englishe pub is not supposed to be. The final insult is to name all the rebuilt bars after historical characters and advertise it as a traditional pub.

The exact age and character of the place doesn't really matter because an instant Olde Englishe outfit can be suppled by the architects, presumably from some vast central warehouse. This will include a framed history of the place written by the brewery's fiction department.

And as regards the traditional English country hotel or inn one of the difficulties these days is finding any English people in them. The weary traveller enters a picturesque little hotel in the main street of some charming village with a name like Adulterating-on-the-Wold and is greeted with a cry of, "You wanna room Senor? OK I get you. Hey, you, Luigi, you getta the gentleman's bags double-quick, hey?" I have even been met in Devon by a hall-porter who didn't speak a word of English and we conversed entirely in signs.

A notice behind the reception desk announces that Consolidated Hotels Ltd. welcome you, and won't be responsible if they lose your baggage. Behind a glass door can be glimpsed a young man in a morning suit who has just been on a training course in Switzerland on how to run a traditional English hotel. He spends his day counting money. And the long-suffering Luigi asks you if "you lika da Engleesh cream tea?"

Fortunately, there are still fine pubs left, both old and new. And some traditional "mine hosts". But the numbers are dwindling. Taxation policies encourage monopoly by big firms and the private owner is priced out, while breweries complete the process by substituting managers for tenants and balance-sheets for hospitality.

Most of the people who talk (and write) glibly about genuine English pubs wouldn't go near a real one; they much prefer the tarted up variety scattered along the banks of the Thames and frequented by people with noisy cars. My idea of a genuine, traditional pub was a little place just off Northampton Market Square, which closed about 15 years ago.

It was a red-brick building about 100 years old with scrubbed deal tables and sawdust on the floor of the public bar. When I was a reporter on the local paper I took a film starlet there to interview her.

She started off by wanting to go into the saloon bar, but I explained that no one used the saloon in hot weather because of the smell and flies from the gents' toilet in the yard. She asked for a gin, but they didn't sell spirits and she had to have shandy. Finally she demanded food—"Not much, just some cold roast beef and salad." I had to tell her that they only had crisps, because Ernie, the landlord, worked in a shoe factory all day and his wife had to cope at lunchtime alone.

At that point Ernie's dog, an ancient hound of bad habits, padded up to the actress, put his head on her thigh and salivated copiously all over her skirt.

"I think this is the grottiest place I've ever been in," she squealed bitterly as she wiped herself down.

The next time I saw her she was taking part in a TV commercial for beer and pretending to knock back halves of wallop "in a typical English pub." Ho, ho.

Nothing sums up the rubbish that surrounds this subject of the traditional pub more than the "ploughman's snack" (a name conjured up by some advertising firm to describe bread and cheese). The only place you can't get a ploughman's snack is in the country. London pubs, however, are full of them.

The quality of a pub is really decided by the man who runs it (be he landlord or manager). A Coarse Drinker must therefore learn how to pick a good landlord and he will be able to choose a good pub. Those who are ignorant of the subject should note, by the way, that in Britain a public-house "landlord" is strictly not a landlord at all, but a tenant of the brewery. However, there is no room to explain the vagaries of the English language, and I shall use the term to mean anyone who runs a public-house, for the sake of simplicity.

It's not easy to decide the quality of a landlord on brief acquaintance; but it is not so difficult to spot a bad guv'nor. A lot can be learned from the way in which he addresses customers. Never patronise a pub where he calls you "Squire" or "friend". Neither have anything to do with the landlord who changes his accent according to the customer he's serving or the part of the country he is in. I met one in Devon who used to have three accents—one for the locals, one for the tourists and one for the lounge-bar. He spoke to the locals in an assumed country dialect: "Ah me old beauty, what you'm be having tonight then?" He addressed visitors in his normal sub-Cockney. And whenever one of the local gentry came into the lounge he put on what he imagined was a middle-class accent and addressed them as "Majah".

My Uncle Walter says he has two golden rules in choosing a pub. He will never patronise one where the toilets have twee names like "Gulls and Buoys" or "Lasses and Lads". And he will never drink in a pub where the landlord calls him "sir".

"Any man, my boy," says Walter, "who is stupid enough to address me as sir, cannot be intelligent enough to run a good public-house."

This is a very wise thought. The term "sir", like the appellation "friend", is a two-edged word. The rudest landlord I ever met used "sir" almost every other word. He threw me out of a bar near Wimbledon Common because he objected to the shortness of my female companion's skirt in the days when the mini was a novelty.

He was one of those men who speak with incredible formality, whatever the occasion, and he ejected me as if he was addressing a House of Lords committee: "Excuse me sir, would you kindly mind asking your good lady-companion if she would have the goodness, sir, either to cover up her knickers or to leave the establishment at once, sir!"

Now the only way to deal with that type is to answer back in the same way. It's no use blustering, or bellowing—that plays right into their hands. The only language they understand is their own convoluted Dornford Yates version of the English tongue.

I replied with a terrible parody of the landlord's manner: "I was always brought up at Charterhouse, sir, to believe, sir, that no gentleman would be so rude, sir, as to comment upon a lady's mode of dress in public, sir!" With a brilliant piece of inspiration I added: "I would not allow it *from any of my constables* and I will not allow it from you."

The last sentence reduced the landlord (who was well-known for serving his cronies after hours) to quivering impotence, and we remained at the bar. Note I did not state the lie that I was a senior police officer. I merely said I would not allow it from one of my constables. And I wouldn't, if I had any constables.

In general, I find the best landlords don't call the customers anything, except by their names, of course. No sirs, guvs, or me-old-beauties. Just nothing—unless you leave the change on the counter, when a small "sir" is permissible.

Although I've described a way of dealing with one type of landlord I don't normally believe it is possible to win an argument with the man behind the bar. He's running the place and if a customer falls out with him the only thing to do is to go. Please pay no attention to public-bar lawyers who claim that publicans are compelled by law to serve everybody. I shall never forget Askew being refused service by a landlord he had quarrelled with, and claiming that under Common Law he was entitled to demand not only beer, but a bed for the night, food, candles and stabling for his horse.

"Unless you serve me," said Askew, "I shall bring a horse into the yard."

"Do so by all means," said the landlord. "I'd far rather serve a horse than you any day. And that goes for your friend too." (The last sentence was a reference to me.)

The landlord's refusal to serve Askew had been dictated by a scurvy trick which Askew had employed on his previous visit. Askew and I had entered the bar and discovered we'd come out without our money.

"Have no fear," said Askew. "I shall cash a cheque."

I pointed to a notice behind the bar, announcing that as the banks had decided not to sell beer, the pubs had agreed not to cash cheques.

Askew smiled quietly, and asked the landlord for two pints of bitter. "And what about your goodself?" he enquired, and the landlord had a light ale. "And your lady-wife?" She had a dry martini. "While you're about it, you'd better get one for Norah in the public." Norah was delighted. "And what about that young couple in the corner? Had a stroke of luck today and I would be honoured if you would help me share it." They, too, were happy to have a gin and tonic each. Eventually this gargantuan round embraced nearly the whole pub, its staff, its customers, and even the landlord's dog, who was bought a packet of crisps.

"That will be two pounds, six and a half," said the landlord after one of those peculiar calculations that only publicans can do. "No—wait a minute, I forget the crisps—two pounds 85 altogether."

"Delighted," says Askew pulling out his cheque-book. "Can you take my note of hand?"

"Sorry sir," said the landlord. "No cheques allowed."

"That is very unfortunate," replied Askew with a mirth-less smile, "as I have no money on me at all. Would you prefer me to write you an IOU or pay you next time?"

After threatening to call the police three times, the publican gave in. Askew's cheque was, in fact, perfectly sound, but I could well understand why we were refused service next time.

But spare a kind thought for the man who runs a pub. Considering the wearing nature of their job, most publicans have incredible patience.

I have served behind a bar and oh! the sight of all those faces demanding, demanding, demanding all the time (and

then painfully counting out their money in slow motion)
and saying oh, they forgot the lemonade and could we have
an eighth-of-an-inch of lime in the light ale—no, only a
strong man or woman can survive. The British barmaid is
living proof of woman's capacity to endure suffering.

One customer I served might well have been trying to
make me insane. He began his order, which came only
after five minutes gibberish about the weather, by asking
for some obscure stuff called Glen Mactavish whisky and
seemed surprised when I said we hadn't got it. He went away
to consult with his friends and when he came back he asked
for a Mist O'Doon whisky. I said we didn't sell that either
but he could have a Haig, which he did. Except that when
I'd poured three double Haigs he said, "Would you mind,
I think we'd rather have gin and tonic instead."

Having sorted all that out, he demanded two pints of a
beer nobody stocked within 100 miles; a French liqueur which
is difficult to get even in France; and a shandy "made with
one-third beer, one-third lemonade, and one-third ginger-
beer."

By the time he'd finished there must have been 10
customers seething with frustration at the lack of service. He
probably cost us far more money than he spent and I would
cheerfully have paid him £5 not to come again.

It is not surprising that some landlords turn into psycho-
paths under the strain and develop peculiarities. I knew one
chap who wouldn't serve salt with the snacks. They were
all home-made by his wife and a request for salt was regarded
as a sort of insult to the cooking.

"Salt?" the landlord would bellow. "How dare you ask
for salt before you've tasted it? How do *you* know how much
salt to put in a shepherd's pie? My wife's been on a catering
course she has, and she knows better than you."

I knew another publican who wouldn't serve Welshmen
(this was before the Race Relations Act). I went into his
place once with a senior official of the Welsh Rugby Union
and as soon as he heard my friend's accent he shouted,
"Get back to Hammersmith you! Don't come trying your
tricks here!" We could never find out what the tricks were,

nor why he always consigned Welshmen to Hammersmith, but the formula never varied.

These used to be a pub near my home where the manager had an obsession about people who tapped on the bar with a coin (it *is* irritating, I must admit). The first time I went there he was busy talking to a customer in the other bar so I tapped a penny on the counter to draw his attention. The landlord ignored it, so I tapped louder and longer. Suddenly he turned and came running into the saloon bellowing and shouting insults.

I was so scared that I hastily turned to go and promptly knocked over a 2 ft pile of pennies on the bar, a charity collection. It was one of the most terrible moments of my life, standing there surrounded by 10,000 pennies on the floor with the landlord gibbering with rage. To make things worse, all his cronies gathered round saying sycophantic remarks like, "Ah, I could see he was going to make trouble the minute he came in, banging on the counter like that . . ." Unfortunately, landlords of that sort can usually count on a small clique of regulars to support them against strange customers.

One of the worse publicans I never met ran a public-house in the Peak District. I say never met because I couldn't even get into the wretched place. A friend and I arrived, thirsty after walking across the hills, at 12.25 one weekday to find it shut. We knocked and nobody answered. But as we stood at the door we saw notices plastered all over the porch:

NO DOGS
NO HIKERS
NO JEANS
NO CLIMBING BOOTS
NO RUCKSACKS

We pencilled underneath "NO SERVICE EITHER" and went on our way. I'm glad we didn't get in as I fear we should not have had a very jovial time.

The experience was, however, a blessing in disguise for two miles further on we came to a pub where we sat by a coal fire drinking pints of bitter and eating enormous ham sandwiches. I have not the slightest intention of revealing its name, either.

A good test of the quality of a landlord is the type of dog which he keeps. I tend to be suspicious of places where a pack of snarling, savage brutes are kept behind the bar and unleashed at closing-time.

One of my more unhappy experiences was when a large Alsatian jumped up from behind the bar and began growling and slavering at me when the landlord called "Time" (they have a marvellous, doggy instinct, it must be admitted, for coming in on cue).

I like dogs and I like them to like me, so I tried to pacify the dog by stretching across the bar counter and patting its head. It replied by seizing the sleeve of my jacket in its fangs, tearing a great hunk of cloth away and chewing it to pieces. Unfortunately, the piece contained a button, which the dog swallowed and was promptly sick. The landlord was absolutely furious.

"How dare you give my dog that button!" he shouted. "You ought to be ashamed of yourself, making a harmless dog ill like that. I've half a mind to set his mate on to you."

I explained that far from feeding my coat to the dog, he had taken it without permission and I would be glad to have it back, including the button, plus compensation for the damage.

"I'll give you damage," was the only reply I got. "I'll report you to the R.S.P.C.A."

The reverse of the Savage Dog Test applies. Landlords who own wheezy old Labradors who crawl round the public bar begging for crisps, usually have their hearts in the right place. A friendly dog means a friendly publican.

So much for publicans. But what about customers? The first thing a Coarse Customer must find out is whether he has a Negative or a Positive Presence. If he has a Positive Presence he will be served, no matter how busy the place is, the minute he enters the door. The barman will look right over the seething throng and take the order as it is mouthed at him. By the time he has reached the bar it will have been poured.

*Negative or Positive presence*

If, on the other hand, he has a Negative Presence, he can stand at the counter, the only person in the whole pub, and still not be served. The barman will either look straight through him; vanish into another bar; or serve someone immediately behind.

The strange thing is that if a Positive Presence merely clears his throat he is immediately served, but a Negative Presence can bang and shout his head off and it won't make any difference. It is all very distressing and speaking as a Negative myself I can offer only one piece of advice: Get someone else to order the drinks. Believe me, no Negative has ever managed to attract barmen or barmaids by *trying*. You've either got it or you haven't, like sex appeal.

Apart from the above, I know only two wheezes for getting on in a public house, but both have been proved extremely useful. One is never to open the door in a hurry (there is a stain on the wall of the Barley Mow, Mayfair, as a result of my forgetting this rule. I opened the door so quickly on a busy night that three people were catapulted across the room along with their respective beers).

The second rule is to beware of any stranger sitting by himself who either offers to buy a drink or tries to start up a conversation. Why is he sitting by himself? Because he is the pub bore. Why is he trying to make conversation to a stranger? Because he can't find anyone else to talk to. Perhaps it's me, but I have never met these interesting strangers in pubs who tell fascinating stories that hold one spellbound. If a man tries to talk to me he invariably turns out to be only interested in getting rid of his life-story, a narrative of hideous dullness. The English public-house is the home of the bore.

### A MERRY MONDAY NIGHT AT THE LOCAL

*A short drama illustrating the joys of the village inn, with apologies to the British Tourist Authority.*

It is 6 p.m. outside a genuine English village pub. The building itself is a former large, redbrick cottage about 150 years old, but this fact has been cleverly disguised by the brewers who have painted it blue and stuck on a flashing neon sign. A car is driven up and a Stranger gets out and looks at his watch. Finding that it is now well past the official opening-hour of six he tries the door. It is locked, and inside all is in darkness. The Stranger sits in his car for a quarter of an hour and tries again. Finding the door still locked, he knocks and is rewarded by a shout from within of "Why don't you ———— off?" After a few minutes, however, the landlord can be heard grumbling and complaining and eventually mine genial host unbars the door reluctantly and the Stranger enters a cold room smelling of stale beer. The darkness is soon dispelled, however, as the landlord switches on a battery of strip lights fitted into the ancient ceiling. The Stranger asks for a pint and the landlord gives him a glass which is twenty per cent foam and so cloudy it is impossible to see through it. The Stranger holds it up to the light and the landlord speaks hastily.

LANDLORD: You won't find anything wrong with that, sir. Pipes were cleaned this morning.

The Stranger thinks better of complaining and sits down. An old man in a muffler comes in, orders half a pint of mild and stares insolently at the Stranger before starting a conversation with the landlord which hasn't varied for 20 years.

OLD MAN: It's a proper booger innit George?

LANDLORD: It is that and all.

OLD MAN: Oi see'd in The Clarion that they boogered them boogers from Birmingham.

LANDLORD: Ah. Some of them boogers want boogering too.

OLD MAN: They do and all. Proper boogers.

This exhausts their conversational powers and silence descends. At this point a young couple enter the deserted lounge next door but finding it in total darkness they leave before the landlord notices them.

A young man named Fred enters the bar and orders a glass of bottled stout. The landlord pours a flat glass with a sour smell and the young man drinks and says that's the stuff innit George, and the landlord agrees. Fred then advances on to a fruit machine which is purring in the corner, awaiting a victim.

STRANGER: [*feeling he ought to make conversation*] I expect you'll be lambing soon.

OLD MAN: Oi shan't, but the sheep will. (He collapses with mirth which turns into a fit of coughing.)

FRED: You ought to be on the telly, you ought.

STRANGER: I expect this is a busy time of the year for you?

OLD MAN: Not for me. Oi work in a garage. Ain't never heard of any sheep owning a car, have you George? (He collapses again.)

The fruit machine makes a noise as if it is about to explode and Fred begins capering about in front of it.

FRED: Oi did it! Oi did it! You see'd 'un George, didn't you? Oi got two of them pictures of a knight in armour and oi held them, and the booger comes up next time on the third line!

LANDLORD: How much have you won?

FRED: Ten pence. And last night oi won five pence, didn't oi George? You see'd me. It's a question of having the right touch.

The Stranger feels he really ought to make a further effort to establish some sort of communication in this traditional old English pub and addresses the landlord again.

STRANGER: Pretty little village you've got here.

LANDLORD: All right if you like that sort of thing I suppose.

STRANGER: Could you please tell me where the toilet is?

LANDLORD: Outside into the road, first left, first left again and you'll find it at the back.

The Stranger goes and returns looking rather dusty.

STRANGER: Excuse me, but do you know there's a car in your toilet?

LANDLORD: You'll cop it—that's the garage.

OLD MAN: Do you 'ear that Fred, this 'ere gentlemen went and did it all over the garage instead of the toilet! Oi bet that didn't do George's car no good!

STRANGER: I didn't do it anywhere. I've come back to ask you where the light is.

LANDLORD: Sorry sir, he don't have a light there. This isn't the Ritz you know.

STRANGER: I know. (He finishes his glass.) I think I'll have a change from beer. Could I have a glass of red wine, an ounce of pipe tobacco, two ham sandwiches and a pickled onion, plus half a bottle of Scotch to take away please?

LANDLORD: Sorry sir, but we don't sell wine, pipe tobacco, sandwiches, pickled onions or half bottles of Scotch. But if it's food you want, we've got some lovely steak pies. Fresh this morning.

He indicates a glass case which contains a solitary plastic-wrapped pie, turned out from its factory a month previously. The Stranger takes it back to his table and bites into it. An expression of anguish spreads over his features as he discovers it consists of a thick coating of dough filled with gristle. He looks for somewhere to hide it.

LANDLORD: Thought you'd enjoy that, sir. You can't beat a bit of good old English cooking.

*The stranger takes it back to his table and bites into it*

A sudden, deafening blast of sound rocks the village, and makes the night hideous for three miles around, as young Fred, tired of the fruit machine, puts money into the juke-box. The landlord, who is apparently impervious to noise, remains unmoved while the Old Man merely nods his head up and down. The Stranger, who is feeling somewhat sick after his pie, and is now being deafened, looks guiltily around for somewhere to hide the remains of the pastry. Failing to find anywhere he stuffs it into the ashtray, nods his farewell and goes out.

LANDLORD: Look at that dirty booger. Left his bleedin' steak pie all over the ashtray. Some people don't deserve to have good food.

OLD MAN: Ah. Oi thought he looked a right dirty booger the moment oi see'd 'un.

Outside the Stranger starts his car and drives hastily to the nearest city. The sixteenth-century clock on the old church tower chimes seven and the gentle sound of the organ is heard across the ancient village green. Harry, the village Romeo, enters the pub.

HARRY: You oughter do something about that there toilet of yourn, George. That danged contraceptive machine be broken again, and oi've got Myrtle waitin' outside.

# 3

# *Special Occasions*

*The Wedding Guest he beat his breast.*

SAMUEL TAYLOR COLERIDGE
Rime of the Ancient Mariner

A true Coarse Drinker is a sociable person and as such he can expect to receive many invitations to special occasions, probably more than he wishes to attend. There is no harm in being selective—nothing is worse than going to functions unwillingly. I never have understood why members of the human race spend so much time going to events which bore them and then inviting their hosts back to something equally vile.

There are two simple Coarse Drinking tests to apply when trying to decide whether to attend a function. They are:

1. How long will the speeches be?
2. How much booze will there be?

At the ideal function the speeches will be brief or non-existent and the drink supply exactly the opposite. The Coarse Drinker should therefore calculate a probably speech/drink ratio based on the number of words spoken compared with drinks consumed.

This ratio should not exceed 500 to one.

Five hundred words is about four minutes speechifying (allowing for pauses etc.) and four minutes is just about as long as one should be expected to listen to a speech before having another drink. If, say, it looks as if there will be three speeches of ten minutes each, then ask yourself if you are likely to get $7\frac{1}{2}$ drinks? This calculation is based on the minimum speech/drink ratio of 500 to one. Three speeches of 10 minutes is equal to approx 3,750 words. Divide by 500 to obtain the *minimum* number of drinks you should get. Or if you like, divide 30 minutes by four.

On this basis many functions fall down immediately. Certainly a lot of weddings do. The one special occasion which almost invariably passes the Coarse Drinking test is, surprisingly enough, the funeral.

My own experience is that hospitality after funerals is much more lavish than at weddings, and there are no speeches at all to spoil the occasion. And everyone is so much more *sociable* than at a wedding. They are more relaxed and talk more. They mix better with strangers.

Anyone who feels guilty at enjoying themselves at a funeral reception can always soothe their consciences with the specious argument, "Charlie would have wanted us to enjoy ourselves", regardless of the fact that Charlie is probably looking down from the Great Saloon Bar up above and gnashing his teeth at the way the guests are knocking back what used to be his private hoard of Scotch.

I remember going to the funeral of an elderly rugby club vice-president. It was a notable occasion, largely because the cars carrying the players followed the wrong hearse, and the guests took part in another funeral before the mistake was discovered. Afterwards the bar takings at the clubhouse were nearly £100 (it was a cold day). There was not one person in that merry throng who didn't say at one time or another, "He would have wanted this, old chap." Nobody remembered that the deceased had been a miserable old sourpuss who didn't drink. Perhaps it was just as well.

In some ways, funerals and weddings have a lot in common. In each case one usually attends a religious ceremony in which a person is being "seen off" to an unknown bourne and a mysterious fate (marriage being quite as big a lottery as survival after death). Handsome public tributes are paid to the people being despatched. Each ceremony involves a lot of standing around in the open air, and while it is quite true that most marriages don't usually require an open grave, my Uncle Walter believes one is not inappropriate at a ceremony which he regards as much sadder than the burial service.

"My boy," he says, "there is not even a hope of resurrection in that terrible marriage service. Not a word of comfort to the unhappy victim."

Plenty of wedding receptions are pretty dismal, too. Occasionally one is invited to a wedding where they have the right ideas about alcohol, but often the unhappy guest has to be content with two glasses of appalling sherry, consumed standing up while trying to balance a plate of cardboard sandwiches.

This is not always the fault of the hosts. I would not describe all outside caterers as being imaginative; and a few are simply cheats, who don't serve all the drink paid for. Duty Number One of any Coarse Drinker whose daughter is getting married, is to see that the guests at least get the drink ordered.

To make matters worse, the guests have to endure this misery for perhaps two hours, and meanwhile listen to speeches with what are meant to be daring jokes about the possibility of children coming along, although everyone knows the happy couple have been sleeping together ever since they were at college, and the bride has had commerce with half the young men in the neighbourhood.

I am not sure that I don't even prefer a genuine teetotal wedding to the sort where drink is available, but in such limited quantities that the little amount served merely tantalises the Coarse Drinker.

Mind you, it takes strong nerves to survive a teetotal wedding. I am one of the few men who has actually attended one, and I cannot describe the anguish of entering the Town Hall for the reception, and seeing vast jugs of lemon squash on the tables. Poor Askew kept hoping to the last that it might prove a ghastly illusion. "Perhaps they're not lemon squash at all," he said desperately. "Perhaps they're gin-and-bitter-lemon. I hear that's the new thing—to serve it in bulk."

But alas, he was wrong. We had already received warning about the ban on alcohol, fortunately, and like all good

*Soon the cloakroom was a seething mass of guests*

Coarse Drinkers we had come prepared for the emergency, and kept slipping away to the cloakroom for a nip. Soon the cloakroom was a seething mass of guests, desperately pulling at flasks and bottles before returning to the torture.

Torture it was, for it is a Law of Coarse Drinking that the less alcohol that is provided at any function, the longer the speeches will last. Where food and drink are lavish the speeches are often reduced to a few muttered words about not losing a daughter but gaining a son. They may be enlivened by the sight of the bride's father sliding under the table as he tries to propose his daughter's health.

Where no drink is on hand, every available relative for hundreds of miles around is dragged to their feet to add to the already endless stream of praise for the happy couple. The teetotal reception just mentioned lasted for three hours.

At least 30 minutes was taken up by the bride's landlady (a distant relative) sobbing and whining about what a good girl she was. Mercifully, she ended her speech with the ambiguous statement that Bridget might have been rather slow in the morning but she was always very good at night.

Further compensation came from the bride's father, who announced loudly, "There will now be an interval while the bride and groom go upstairs and put their things together."

I must say I thought I was going to choke.

The curse of a wedding is the practical joke, which may range from tying kippers on the bridegroom's exhaust pipe to telegraphing the honeymoon hotel and cancelling the reservation. Personally, I always regard this sort of thing as a sign that there wasn't enough to drink. Satan makes mischief for idle hands to do, and no one should bother with silly japes if there's still plenty of champagne floating around.

The Coarse father-in-law has therefore two actions to perform to avoid the jokers: firstly, to provide as much drink as possible; and secondly, to obtain a dummy going-away car as a decoy for any jests. For the decoy-car look no further than the long-suffering best man.

Should the vicar be invited to a wedding reception? Yes, if he promises to take off that silly collar. I have never yet known an occasion of joy which wasn't ruined by the sight of that ridiculous back-to-front collar leering at everyone. It's not the presence of a vicar that worries people at parties, it's his collar.

Catholic priests pose a slightly different problem. I have never known a body of men with such a vast appetite for food and drink as the Catholic priesthood. It must be ingrained from the Church's tradition of the persecution of the faithful—they feel that at any minute the revolution may come, so they're going to stuff themselves while there's time. If a priest is invited allow for three extra places.

Keep any well-filled priest away from elderly aunts. Tipsy priests have a knack of starting to tell jokes about nuns which are great fun but rather embarrassing to some people.

While the presence of clergy can add much to a wedding reception it can bring problems. As when Askew's eldest daughter, Angela, got married and the reception was held at her father's home. Askew's provision of hospitality was, I need hardly add, lavish and no one participated more generously than Askew himself. After two hours everything was going splendidly when the vicar mentioned to Askew that he played golf.

"By George," bellowed Askew. "That is a coincidence. Between you and me vicar, Angela was actually conceived on the third fairway at Wentworth."

A ghastly silence fell on the party. The good vicar turned pale and started to back away at this alarming piece of information but there was no stopping the drunken Askew now.

"Well, you know what youth is, vicar," he blundered on. "We were only youngsters at the time and it was dark you know." He gave a ghastly leer and nudged the vicar in the ribs. "Of course we never told you when we had her christened. I mean there is a code, you know."

Worse was to follow. Seized by an alcoholic desire to unburden himself, Askew began dragging the vicar around the house, pointing out the various places in which he alleged his children had been conceived (they ranged from the spare bedroom to the lounge floor, not to mention the marital bed).

The vicar stood it as long as he could but eventually fled rather suddenly while Askew was pointing out a particularly bizarre place of conception behind the bathroom door.

"I wonder if I have offended him in some way?" mused Askew. "I don't think I should have told him about what happened on the third fairway you know. After all, I wasn't a member at the time, and if the vicar's a golfer he probably feels a bit upset about it. But surely he doesn't expect me to have paid a green fee?"

## Christenings

In my experience, christenings are not really an occasion for great joviality or drinking. I don't know why this should be, unless it is the hour at which they are usually performed (although both funerals and weddings take place at peculiar drinking hours, and can be quite festive affairs).

Perhaps it is the influence of the godparents, who having been in church for the first time in 15 years are feeling rather overawed by the occasion. Especially as they have just made a series of ludicrous vows about giving up the lusts of the flesh and feel they ought to make some sort of pretence at doing so. They are also probably rather worried as to whether committing adultery counts as a lust of the flesh; and if so, whether this means the child can't go to Heaven because it's not properly christened.

Uncle Walter used to produce a christening punch but gave it up because nobody really felt like drinking. Or perhaps it was the punch. However, I give the recipe:

## Uncle Walter's Christening Punch

Ingredients: One half-bottle gin, three bottles white wine, one bottle benedictine. A little fruit. Lots and lots and lots and lots of ice. Stir. Serve very cold. NOTE: See Author's warning at the beginning of this book.

### Birthdays

I can never understand why anyone over the age of 40 wants to celebrate a birthday. Birthdays are fine for the young, but why should one celebrate when Time's Wingèd Chariot is not merely hovering near, but parked outside the door and sounding its horn?

Why make merry about the fact that mind and body have aged one year more and the inevitable progress to the tomb has increased by 365 days? To add insult to injury the unfortunate person thus afflicted is expected to buy other people drinks to celebrate his own decay.

It is even worse if one was born in the early hours, because you spend the whole night tossing and groaning and looking at the clock and wondering "Am I one year older yet?" and wishing the clock could be put back. Drink merely makes the whole thing worse, because in addition to the mental misery you wake up with a hangover, feeling not merely one year older but ten years older, and probably looking it as well.

Here is a Coarse Drinking warning: Never be tempted by birthday booze to prove that the years have really wrought no change, that one is just as strong, hale and lusty as ever. Thus did a distant relative celebrate his fiftieth year by leaping into a swimming pool fully-clad at midnight. Unfortunately it was empty, but he was soon walking again with the aid of two sticks.

Nothing is sadder than a middle-aged man boasting on his birthday that he wouldn't want to be twenty again, he was even more successful now with sport, women etc. than ever before.

Birthdays over the age of 40 should be celebrated by a private dinner party at which one invites all one's elderly friends, preferably those in bad health. A good rule is that no one should be younger than the host. I always find it helps to invite people who have had unhappy lives and encourage them to talk about their troubles.

"And has your son come out of prison yet?" I ask, pushing the port forward. "It must be a bitter disappointment to you. I expect it has ruined your whole life, hasn't it?"

Having thus cheered myself with someone else's tale of woe I may pass on to another guest with some innocent comment like "It must be rotten to reach middle-age and know that you will never get any further promotion in your career."

Thus the merry evening passes, with the guests moaning and regretting their lost chances and their rotten lives, so that by the end of it all I feel quite cheerful in contrast.

Under the age of 40, birthdays might be a suitable occasion for celebration since the following year may well bring increased health, wisdom and wealth (which is certainly not true as you get older). It is a pity that the age of majority has now been brought down to 18, since the old 21st birthday party provided a splendid opportunity for celebration. Eighteen is perhaps too young to appreciate what is involved, and at that age one is almost certainly too inexperienced in drink to gain the full benefit.

It is a strange coincidence that the same dangers apply to the coming-of-age celebration as apply to the middle-aged birthday party. The young want to prove they're men, and the middle-aged want to prove they're young.

In each instance the temptation to do so should be removed. All that the celebrant usually manages to prove is that he is completely whiffled.

## Christmas

Personally, I have always held the view that Scrooge was a much misunderstood man. But then it is typical of the hypocrisy that surrounds our modern, commercially-orientated Christmas, that this sensible, hard-working, moderate person, who merely disliked the disturbance which Christmas caused to his domestic and business routine, should be held up as an example of everything that's vile.

The fact is, that a great many people would say "I hate Christmas" if they weren't scared of being labelled Scrooges. The trouble with the secular aspect of Christmas (as distinct from the religious side) is that it is a mediaeval junket which has become a positive burden in modern times.

In Scrooge's era, Christmas was not merely the only holiday of the year, it was probably the only occasion on which some of the poor got a decent meal. In an age when Lancashire cotton workers lived on potatoes and bacon fat Christmas stood out as a beacon of good cheer in the middle of the long winter.

Today, most people stuff themselves so much with food and drink all year round, that we attempt the impossible on Christmas Day and try to stuff ourselves even further. The worst aspect is the compulsory boozing. I like a drink. In fact I like six or seven. But I like to take them when I want them, not to have them forced down my throat because it's December.

For something like a week before Christmas Day, the unhappy reveller totters from one drink to another, a

ghastly smile of fake joviality painted on the face, behind
which it feels as if the Battle of Agincourt is being fought by
little men. And all the hospitality comes at such odd hours.

You call on a neighbour at 8.30 a.m. to return a lawn-
mower and he forces great tumblers of whisky on you. You
drop round on a pal for coffee at ten-fifteen and he makes you
drink a pint of Bass.

In offices all intelligent work ceases a week before Christmas, largely because the senior staff are pressing triple gins
on each other at unlikely times such as 4 o'clock in the
afternoon. Could you believe it, but I once called on a
business acquaintance, who forced a pint of draught
Guinness down me at 9.25 a.m.?

"It's Christmas," he said as if that explained everything.

Strangely enough, teetotallers are among the worst
offenders at plying people with unwanted drink. They
haven't the faintest idea of the customary amount to dispense,
or what it tastes like or when it should be served, or what its
effect is, but they don't want to feel out of things so they err
on the side of safety and generosity.

A teetotaller's idea of "a little nip as it's the festive
season" is a filthy great goblet of whisky, probably pressed
on the unwilling victim at some unlikely hour such as
breakfast-time.

Old ladies are the biggest menaces. I shall never forget
what happened when an elderly landlady served me a
tumblerful of neat crême-de-menthe to drink with birthday
cake and tea.

"I never touch a drop myself," she said firmly, "as you
well know Mr. Green, although Mr. Haddock used to
like a brown ale on New Year's Eve when he was alive. But
I know you like a little drop occasionally." (She was right
there, I liked a good deal more than a drop, but I preferred
it during normal drinking hours, not with my tea.)

However, I forced a smile and pretended to be pleased
when she handed me a pint tumbler full to the brim of
crême-de-menthe. And dear Lord, it was *warm*.

My attempts merely to sip gently at this while coping with
the iced cake upset her and she anxiously asked if it was all

right, as she didn't know about these things. It was the only drink she had in the house, having been there since her husband's funeral. A garish picture arose in my mind of the mourners sitting round a bottle of crême-de-menthe in black top hats.

I didn't want to offend her, so I decided on emergency measures. I stood up, toasted her health, tilted back my head, drained the tumbler of crême-de-menthe in one go and muttered the traditional "Ah . . ."

For a moment I felt better. I had got the worst over and was now ready for flight. But then I stood up to reach for the sugar and caught sight of the mirror on the wall. What appeared to be a blue-faced man was gibbering and grimacing in it. I hastily sat down, but unfortunately missed my chair by two feet and ended up on the carpet, taking the egg-and-cress sandwiches with me.

I quickly murmured some excuse and hastily tried to leave the room, but they seemed to have papered over all the doors and twice I tried to go through the cupboard before I eventually succeeded in blundering into the hall. After demolishing a rack full of overcoats I finally made my bedroom, where I lay in a coma for twelve hours.

Strange perversity of human nature, my landlady afterwards blamed *me* for the whole thing.

*What appeared to be a blue-faced man was gibbering and grimacing in it*

"It's getting a grip on you, Mr. Green," she said severely the next day, when I tottered downstairs. "My cousin went like that. They had to give him brandy on his death-bed, he needed alcohol so much." Personally I think the poor chap was probably quite all right until his birthday.

Incidentally, it is strange how the older generation all had relatives who died of drink. I haven't met one person over 70 who hasn't a family story of Cousin Bill or Uncle Jeremy who got in the grip of the demon alcohol, but who still had the strength to die crying, "What will become of the little ones?" Most of the little ones appeared to grow up quite well, however.

The compulsory Christmas joviality reaches its height on Christmas Eve. I think I can say that normally I like pubs. But for the life of me I can't see why anyone goes to one on Christmas Eve. Everyone has to stand packed like pilchards, without even room to blow a nose, beer is swilling all over the place, it takes ten minutes to get served, there's a fight going on in the public bar and by golly, it's all *compulsory*. By that, I mean the social habit is so strong one doesn't really think of doing anything else. Besides, you'd feel left out of things if you didn't conform.

In my opinion the only decent place in a pub on Christmas Eve is under the bar billiard table (if any) with a crate of light ale or a bottle of Scotch. And even then, you'd find someone's dog had got there first.

(I ought to confess, perhaps, at this point, that my prejudice against Christmas Eve partly stems from the time when I upset a tray containing nine pints of bitter on Dec 24, 1951, at the old Nag's Head Inn, Leicester. This simple act, caused by the crush, managed to ruin something like six people's suits and their Christmas's as well. The landlord, banned me for six months after that and I had to use the Royal Standard.)

The result of all this enforced conviviality is that Christmas Day itself, which should be the happiest day of the year, is a time of bloated gloom. The family lie around in a daze after lunch, the silence being broken only by the odd belch or the occasional cry of pain from an elderly member of the party.

Besides compulsory drinking, compulsory entertaining is another hazard of Christmas. Simply because it is Christmas one is expected to invite people of unutterable boredom.

To make things worse, it is impossible to stop visitors coming simply by giving them an awful time. They seem to accept that Christmas is terrible anyway, and don't expect to enjoy themselves. In any case, they probably don't know how to. With the result that the house is crammed with bored people who have all eaten and drunk too much. Even those who haven't overdone it—such as a puritanical aunt—will be in a mood of stern disapproval that's as bad as indigestion.

There is, however, a Coarse Drinking Wheeze which will put a stop to some compulsory entertaining. It is based on the fact that the only way to stop these people coming is to *overdo the hospitality*.

Ah, strange paradox of existence that while most of the human race are so dull they can stand any amount of futile boredom (such as the telly), most of them curl up when a good time is offered. So, to rid the house of unwanted guests simply ply them with food and drink. Lash out the whisky at 5 o'clock, together with a plate of something highly indigestible such as macaroons (I'm never quite sure what a macaroon is—it sounds like something for calling out the lifeboat, but I know it's indigestible).

Repeat at half-past five and six o'clock. They'll be gone by half-past and with any luck won't return next year. NOTE: It is difficult for guests to refuse hospitality. The same iron law that says you have to entertain them at Christmas also says you are entitled to press unlimited food and drink on them.

Askew banished a much-hated relative of his wife's by inviting the darts team from his local pub to his house at three o'clock in the afternoon and opening a barrel of draught beer. The unfortunate relative turned green by six and had to be driven home.

Of course, guests must still be invited the following year, under Christmas entertaining regulations. But if the wheeze described is employed, with luck they may reply: "I think we'd better stay home this year. Donald felt so awful last time." (And no wonder after being forced to consume cherry brandy and toast at half-past five.)

Faced with the menace of compulsory Christmas merriment, a Coarse Drinker is entitled to defend himself with any weapons he can find (the anti-boozing wheeze). On December 21 start clutching the bosom and announce it's funny, you had a stabbing pain and you hope it's nothing, as you don't want to spoil Christmas, ho, ho, ho. On December 23 clutch the bowels and say it's strange, but there's that pain again and you hope you're not going to have internal trouble with the festive season coming.

On December 24, preferably in the canteen at lunchtime, clutch chest, stomach, and bowels all at once and stagger out making retching noises. Leave in a taxi having phoned home to say you have been taken ill. Thus at office and home you are established as a sick man, excused compulsory drinking parades.

On December 28 return to work fit and well, to be faced with a terrible parade of colleagues—white-faced men, pallid office girls wondering if anyone will find out what they got up to, married women who've aged ten years over the holiday.

You will probably be the only person who's actually enjoyed Christmas. And then you can get back to some genuine Coarse Drinking.

**4**

# Drinking and Business

> Sir Christopher Wren
> Said, "I am going to dine with some men.
> If anybody calls
> Say I am designing St. Pauls."
>
> E. C. BENTLEY

Among the more monotonous aspects of newspapers every Christmas is a column headed How to Survive the Office Party, and decorated by a photograph of what appears to be a prison matron, but which turns out to be the female journalist who wrote it. This column will be devoted entirely to warning girls on the perils of the party—both sexual and alcoholic—and how to avoid them. Most of the advice is quite useless and consists of stupid homilies like "Don't allow a man to offer to do up your zip."

This is typical of the sort of drinking myth which the Coarse Drinker must see through. After all, everyone *knows* what the office party is going to be like. The whole point of it is for people to let their hair down. The girls don't *want* to avoid the office wolves. Most of them are only too happy to get a little high and giggly at the firm's expense. Expecting circumspect behaviour at the office party is like expecting a girl to remain pure at a university.

I am baffled as to why female journalists—a class not particularly known for either their sobriety or their chastity— should indulge in such hypocrisy. I shall therefore offer no advice like "sip the punch slowly" or "never go into the broom cupboard with the Sales Manager." Especially as it might prove rather interesting in there. But I must offer certain wheezes for the Coarse Drinkers who are career-conscious because office parties are one of the most important aspects of Business Drinking. They can have more effect on a person's life than success or failure in an examination.

Let it be stated immediately—many people who are sacked, or passed over for promotion in July, don't realise that it is a direct result *of the office party in December.*

Think back. Did you say anything unwise? Did you lurch up to the Sales Manager and say, "The trouble with you ol' man, is that you don't know anything about selling?" Did you tell the General Manager your private scheme for re-organisation, which involved abolishing him? If so, shudder. And do not fool yourself that they were too merry to remember. One of the things that distinguishes top management from ordinary men is that they *always* remember what was said no matter how much they had to drink.

Remember, too, that flattery is as bad as insult. It is just as dangerous to put an arm round the Managing Director and say, "I want you to know, old bean, that I think you're just the greatest little boss in the world," as it is to punch him on the nose.

Neither is drink the only enemy. In the free-and-easy atmosphere be careful which women you approach. To seduce successfully the Chairman's secretary will without a shadow of doubt infuriate him. After all, either he has successfully done the same in which case he will be jealous; or else he hasn't but wanted to, in which case he will be equally jealous.

Remember that middle-aged business executives have strange fantasies. Successful wooing of the most unlikely typist, or even the office cleaner, may offend someone in authority who has lusted after her furtively for years.

It must have been some such episode which led to my being dismissed from a job some fifteen years ago. When I returned to work after the office party everyone looked at me in a strange way, and all the girls giggled.

"Good morning," said the commissionaire. "Are you feeling normal now?" And he added rather sinisterly: "If you are going up in the lift, would you like me to put a chair in it for you? I expect you're feeling pretty exhausted . . . ."

My boss's secretary, a rather larky young girl, pretended to flatten herself against the wall in fear when I got to my room, and a colleague commented, "Well, well, I'm glad to see you made it. Thought we might never see you again."

Yet the worst of it was, I couldn't remember what I was supposed to have done. I never did find out. Even the commissionaire wouldn't tell me. It must have been some dreadful social gaffe which I didn't realise I'd made, such as mistaking one of the new directors for the man who came to clear the drains. Or did I have a black-out for 5 minutes and dance naked on the desks? All I do know, is that shortly afterwards I was fired on some trivial pretext. When I protested the boss said mysteriously, "I don't suppose it's exactly a surprise after what happened at the party."

The Coarse Drinker had better decide, therefore, that if he is going to the office party at all he had better follow certain rules, or not go. These rules include:

Lock your own office, unless you want to find couples writhing all over the desk.

Lock the filing cabinet unless you want someone (a) to read the files, (b) be sick in it.

(*Note:* One of the peculiarities of the Office Party is that a person is blamed for what happens in his own office, whether he did it or not. It's no use being as pure as a lamb if someone else is found with a girl in your office. Somehow the owner of the office will be considered as having committed the deed himself.)

Leave any wooing of women until afterwards. It is best to make an assignation with them in a pub round the corner. Then no jealousies are aroused.

Keep conversation with those senior to yourself away from business and sex. Do not boast of amorous exploits to the bosses. Feign purity.

Do not be absent from the room longer than possible. People get suspicious if you disappear.

If you find the Sales Manager in the broom cupboard with his secretary, simply say: "I'm sorry, I thought this was the lift," and go at once.

And remember—a business executive is never off-duty. That also goes for Generals, headmasters, university Professors and anyone in authority. It's a hall-mark of rank.

(Aunty Gladys has just told me she thinks it disgusting to write about girls having too much to drink at office parties. But Uncle Walter said: "Pay no attention to her, my boy. She has forgotten how when she was a lady typist before the war she had too much sherry at the office party. She wouldn't stop laughing and one of the clerks had to travel back in the train to Croydon with her to see she got home all right. I know, because, it was me. I held her hand all the way from Clapham Junction. And in those days, that was as far as you would get with a girl for a long time.")

Another form of Coarse Business drinking is the office farewell to a retiring member of the staff. By this, I don't mean retirement ceremonies of the official sort, with the managing director wishing the retiring employee a long and happy retirement, and probably thinking to himself that he'll be lucky to live 12 months on that pension.

This is followed by the presentation of a gold watch, or briefcase, and the speech in reply, and the strained laughter, and then perhaps the big surprise! Yes, behold, three bottles of Cyprus sherry are being wheeled into the office by genial, fat Mrs. Wallace of the canteen, and everyone can have a genial, fat glass, except the managing director, who can't face the stuff and hastens away to spend £20 of the shareholder's money on lunching a friend.

No, the Coarse Retirement ceremony usually involves an office farewell to someone either sacked or moving to another firm. There is nothing official about it and the ceremony is conducted by the leaver's colleagues.

The normal routine on these occasions is for the happy leaver to adjourn to the nearest pub on the lunchtime of his last day and to hold court for his office friends. I see no way of bettering this excellent routine but the departing one must beware of the expense involved in buying twenty or thirty rounds of drinks. This is unfair, and the rule must be that the leaver is only expected to buy everybody one drink.

*The leaver is only expected to buy everybody one drink*

Otherwise his entire accumulated pension fund rights will vanish in two hours.

An interesting aspect of these unofficial farewell ceremonies is the way in which the leaver's attitude changes during the lunch-hour. At one o'clock he's full of bounce and confidence and glad to be quitting this rotten hole; by three o'clock it's what a good chap Charlie's been and I'll come back and see you all ever so often won't I?

Every lunch-time leaving party invariably ends with a hard core of people ejected on to the pavement at closing-time, arguing about where they can get more tipple. If in this situation, never believe the man who thinks he can get you in the back door of a certain bar, or who knows a club where he's certain non-members are served if you ask nicely.

Ignore the fantasies, as in all Coarse Drinking. It's a wise man who knows when the party's over.

If a guest, pay no heed to anything said or done during leaving parties. Old wounds may re-open and bitter words be said: forget them. The leaver will almost certainly offer most of his pals a job ("Just give me a few days and I'll fix you up as my assistant"). Forget it. He may offer to lend you money or fix you up with a woman; worse, he may offer an embarrassing confidence, putting his arm round your shoulder and muttering, "Actually old chap, I wouldn't tell anybody else, but now I'm leaving I don't mind letting you know that it was me who pinched the office tea-money last year. Put it on a horse and it lost."

Never, never, never refer to such matters again. Do not ring up and ask for the job, the money or the woman. In any case, the leaver will already have forgotten who you are. Do not go round telling everybody that Fred pinched the tea-money. Anything said at a farewell office party is to be forgotten at once. It's mostly fantasy anyway.

Added spice is given to a farewell party if the leaver has been sacked or has left with a grievance. There is a delicious sense of anticipation in wondering what he's going to do when the pub closes.

Most leavers who have been fired spend the morning telling everyone what they are going to say or do to the boss after lunch, and then spend the afternoon failing to do it. I remember a fellow-reporter on a provincial newspaper who on being dismissed swore he would return to the office after his farewell, enter the editor's room, and spit on his desk. He left the pub waving his arms and issuing threats and actually got as far as bursting into the editor's office. The editor was dictating a letter to his secretary. Her version later was that the angry reporter's courage deserted him and he merely stammered that he had come to say goodbye, to which the editor replied, "Shut the door as you go out."

The reporter's story, which became an office legend, was a wild yarn in which the cringing editor was leaping about the room dodging a shower of spit. Such is human nature, we all believed the reporter's lunatic version.

A more successful farewell gesture on the same newspaper was by a reporter who celebrated his departure by inserting a totally false and embarrassing piece of news about the Mayor in the paper's gossip column. But in time the editor became cunning and witheld the pay of anyone leaving until Friday afternoon, as a form of blackmail. He also took the precaution of keeping out of the way all day.

This, however, did not stop a dismissed photographer pasting a copy of the Sermon on the Mount on the editor's door, with the passages relating to the poor and the meek heavily underlined.

Generally speaking, however, guests at a leaving party should have no part in any move by the host to contact his former bosses. Beware of the lunchtime mob orator, with his half-baked ideas like, "Let's all go back and sing the Red Flag outside the Managing Director's door, lads." People like this have a habit of disappearing at the vital moment, and the Coarse Drinker may well find himself standing there bellowing about the workers' flag alone, when the managing director marches out to see who is making all the noise.

Once the party is over say goodbye and become invisible. And if the leaver insists on lurching round the office all afternoon, pretend you don't know him. A senior executive who finds you supporting him in the corridor may well come to the conclusion that it's time *you* held *your* leaving party.

Like the office party, a Coarse Drinker must also treat with care a firm's or departmental dinner. All the rules mentioned previously for the office party apply, with two additional ones:

1. Never organise the dinner. 2. Never speak at it (or offer to provide a speaker).

I have never yet known anyone praised for organising a good dinner. The hotel or restaurant always get the credit if things go right. But if they go wrong, the organiser is blamed for everything, right down to the cloakroom attendant. As regards speaking, the same you-can't-win rule applies. If you are witty, you'll offend someone; if you're serious, everyone says what a dull speech. Note that the organiser takes the blame for any speakers he invites, but the speakers take any credit if they are successful.

Fortunately, it's not very difficult to find someone to organise a business dinner, so there should be little trouble in avoiding the job. Some people imagine that the organiser has nothing to do except stand around in a dinner jacket and win instant promotion. I recall a young and ambitious area sales manager who volunteered to run the reps' annual dinner in London, and as his *coup* produced for guest speaker a famous sports writer.

There was an air of expectancy as the famous commentator stood up to speak. The expectancy became a little strained, however, when he stood there swaying for two minutes without being able to articulate a word, owing to the fact that he was utterly honked. Suddenly the journalist let out a word which proved to be "Leonard." There was a further ghastly silence for another 60 seconds, during which his face could be seen working with effort, and he then produced the word "Hutton". At this rate his speech would have gone on for fourteen hours, so they tried to make him sit down. Even then it took three minutes of tugging at his coat before he'd shut up, during which he managed to get out one more word—"was". After sitting down, he sat beaming at everybody and nodding as if he'd just made the speech of his life. The area sales manager was not promoted.

Another aspect of business drinking that must be mentioned is the business lunch. I find it difficult to understand why so many businessmen find it impossible to get through the afternoon's work unless they are utterly and completely bottled, but that is not my problem. I always accept lunches gratefully, even though some publishers come to the end of the meal having forgotten what we were supposed to discuss.

The publishing trade is notorious for its lunches but it took me some time to work up to the free meal which is usually given to every author. Indeed, when my first book was accepted, almost the first words after signing the contract were: "Can I have my lunch now?"

Unfortunately, as nobody thought the book would ever sell, I didn't get it. I waited and waited for the call, but it never came, until one day I looked in on my publisher unexpectedly with an urgent correction.

I apologised if I had made him late for lunch.

"Not a bit of it," he boomed. (Some publishers actually do boom. I always think "boomed like a publisher" would be more appropriate than "boomed like a bittern".) "Why don't you join me in a bite?"

In my innocence I presumed that The Call had come. I was to have My Lunch. I said I'd love to.

"Jolly good," replied my publisher and produced a brown paper bag containing tomato sandwiches. "Have one of these. My wife makes them."

I remember being so angry that I determined to gain my revenge. I wrote three articles and two radio talks about the meanness of publishers but he never saw or listened to them. "Did you hear my broadcast about publishers the other day?" I'd say, and he'd say what a pity, he must have missed it, was it very funny? No, I used to say, it was bitter and tragic.

A final business drinking hazard—showing the Town to visiting customers or colleagues. This is especially dangerous in London because all the visitors want to see the sin, and the "sinful" places in London are so dreary no Londoner ever goes there (largely because it's all pay and no sin). Yet visitors still insist on being dragged along to pay triple prices for their drinks and then nudge and ask "what about the girls, eh?" If they genuinely wanted sex they'd do far better to go to a dance at Kensington Town Hall and pick up some bored young schoolteacher, but all they really want is the fantasy.

I have even been on a business trip to Scunthorpe, of all places, with a colleague who after dinner spent the whole evening trying to find a strip club and *actually succeeded,* although I think it took him a twenty-mile drive. ("Most interesting", Uncle Walter has just commented. "I never knew there was a strip club near Scunthorpe. Do you have the address?")

Unless one likes being robbed by paid hostesses as a substitute for sex, it is difficult to enjoy the compulsory sin.

patrol for visitors. The only suggestion I can make is to take them somewhere pleasant and pretend it is a den of vice. Could one take them to a concert at the Festival Hall under the pretext that all the women in the orchestra were going to strip naked at the end of Beethoven's Ninth? I doubt it.

But I did manage to bring one particularly dreary evening to a premature close. I was entertaining three bald-headed men from Huddersfield who had dragged me through every clipjoint in Soho. I had just calculated that my entertainment allowance had run out and any further expense would have to be on me.

There were three club hostesses at the table when a photographer snapped the group and started to take orders.

"Run for your lives!" I cried. "He's a blackmailer. Nowhere in London is safe from them!"

The three guests rose vertically and fled, holding paper napkins over their faces. I must try that again sometime.

*"Run for your lives!" I cried. "He's a blackmailer"*

# 5 *Parties and Entertaining*

*And when Yourself with silver Foot
shall pass
Among the Guests Star-scattered on
the grass*

RUBAIYAT OF OMAR KHAYYAM

The greatest mistake made about parties is to think guests are going to be grateful to their hosts, and that an expensive party will win friends and influence people favourably.

Such is the contrariness of human nature, to which I may have already referred occasionally, that no one is the least grateful to you for spending £50 entertaining them, and putting up with red wine stains ruining the carpet and cigarette ends burning great holes in the furniture.

The Coarse Drinker must realise that often there will be little gratitude, apart from the mechanical thanks-so-much-for - a - lovely - time - and - we're - so - sorry - Fred - burned - the - tablecloth - with - his - cigar - ha - ha - ha - type of farewell. Instead, the majority of the guests will be indulging in an orgy of carping and criticism as soon as they are out of earshot.

(*Note:* Anyone who values peace of mind should never linger at the front door as the guests depart. Some of them are so eager to start complaining, they don't wait until they can't be heard, and the host may catch an unpleasant reference to him or herself.)

There is no need to be depressed by this, however. That is the purpose of a formal party, or Posh Nosh as I like to call it. The idea is to give enjoyment to people, and if some of the enjoyment comes in discussing the party afterwards, why complain? If one sets out the stall, you must expect people to criticise the goods.

The more lavish the party, the more lavish the criticism. A friend of mine once gave a champagne party. Unlike most alleged champagne parties, at which guests receive one miserable glass of bubbly before it runs out, this was genuine. Champagne flowed until 4 a.m., by which time most of the guests were flowing too.

Next day I overheard a neighbour say to another: "Personally, I thought it was all rather ostentatious." And the speaker was a man who had nearly bathed in free champagne all night. In fact he'd had the cheek to use it to sponge a stain off his coat.

So, if it's friendship and gratitude you're after, then the Coarse Drinker must realise that this comes in inverse proportion to the lavishness of the party. In fact far more kind words are likely to be generated if some unforeseen disaster such as illness ruins the occasion.

A Coarse Drinker who is really determined to succeed as a host or hostess might well take this lesson to heart and throw a non-party for a change. Let me explain.

Invitations are sent out in the normal way and the guests assemble. But they don't find a carefully-arranged room with bowls of peanuts, soft lighting, a smiling host and a ravishing hostess. Instead, they find chaos. A vacuum cleaner is on the carpet, children's toys on the stairs. The host hasn't changed. The hostess is nowhere to be seen.

Things are explained by the host's greeting: "I'm sorry for the mess but Daphne's in bed. She twisted her ankle hanging up the washing this afternoon . . ." (Useful alternatives are she had a stroke, saved three children from drowning, got hurt stopping a runaway horse, etc., etc.)

The guests express sympathy and prepare to go. Now play the Master Wheeze.

"No, no. Daphne insists you don't go" (a feeble squeak is heard from upstairs). "We've got a bottle of Scotch and if we rummage in the fridge we can find some ham and a few bottles of hock."

Within half-an-hour the party will be steaming along, everyone sitting on the floor, munching enormous sandwiches, swigging Scotch out of tumblers and roaring with laughter.

At this point a faint moaning may be heard outside the door and the hostess totters in, leaning on a stick (or hopping on a crutch, clutching her chest, retching continually, according to what disability she is supposed to have). She asks in a croaking voice, "Are things really too awful?"

A roar of denial greets her. "No, no couldn't be better . . . Harry's a wonderful host . . . have something to drink . . ."

"Well, just a little one . . . OUCH!" (her ankle/heart/pelvis gives way). She is tenderly helped to a chair and revived with a small drink.

Have no doubt of the success of the Non-Party. The same people who will criticise a pretentious party will come round to the host's side if they think he's not trying to go one better in The Great Battle of Life. There's nothing like seeing someone in trouble for making people feel superior, un-threatened, and therefore sympathetic. The Non-Party brings out the best in human nature; the Posh Nosh brings out the worst.

Fancy dress parties have certain advantages. They tend to make people shed inhibitions and mix easily. The costumes help pairing off. Indeed, I first met Askew through going to a fancy dress party as Napoleon, to find that his sister Maureen had come as Josephine. Any budding romance was, however, nipped in the bud by Askew coming up and saying loudly, "You're wasting your time there, old man."

I went as Napoleon merely because the local dramatic society happened to have a Napoleon costume spare. But one of the fascinations of fancy dress is that people wear a costume that reveals their secret desires. Thus elderly matrons may go dressed as Maid Marion; and downtrodden clerks as Adolf Hitler.

Lack of a costume need be no bar to a Coarse Drinker wishing to attend a fancy dress party. The simplest thing is to go in one's own clothes and announce firmly, "I am disguised as a drunken, shabby middle-aged man."

Tramp suppers are another version of fancy dress, although they always fill me with a sense of social guilt. If you've

*"I am disguised as a drunken, shabby middle-aged man"*

even seen a *real* tramps' supper on some vacant site in South London, with the poor chaps swigging methylated spirits and gibbering to themselves, one can't help feeling that it's not exactly something to romanticise by putting burnt cork on your face. But from the Coarse Drinker's point of view, it does breed an air of informality. As for the host, he can get away with serving beer and sausages instead of more expensive stuff, on the grounds of realism. One could, of course, always serve a genuine tramp's cocktail of meths and cyder and see what happens.

Tennis clubs seem particularly prone to tramp suppers, perhaps because their members have never seen a tramp. I shall always remember one such occasion at a select tennis club, which was completely ruined by the appearance of a *genuine* tramp. We noticed this man with a long beard down to his waist and dressed in an old Army greatcoat tied with string but everyone thought he was a guest. In fact, most members decided he had rather overdone it, and did not deserve a prize.

He rejected all attempts at conversation and spent the entire evening absolutely stuffing himself with food at the buffet, and then disappeared. His identity was only dis-covered when the caretaker came in next day and found him asleep in the boiler room under a pile of old clothes, sur-rounded by pork-pie crusts.

What is the test of a good party? Askew's Rule says a good party is one at which you can't remember what happened. Be that as it may (whatever that means), simple entertain-ment is the most appreciated. At one of the finest dinner-parties I ever attended the host had merely provided a joint of under-done Scotch beef, some lettuce, hot rolls and butter, and about five gallons of draught cider, poured into jugs with ice, the whole being served in his garden on a hot summer's evening.

Askew has even held a dinner-party without food, and I must say it was one of the best I have known. In fairness, he had intended to have food but while guests were sipping aperitifs there came a loud bang from the kitchen and his wife rushed in without any eyebrows, from which we deduced there had been a gas explosion. What was left of the dinner was promptly ruined by a man who flooded the kitchen with foam from a fire-extinguisher.

One could not help but admire Askew.

"The wine is still safe!" he cried triumphantly from under the stairs, while guests fought the flames. Eventually we all gathered back in the living-room where Askew served us sherry which we should have poured into the soup. That was followed by Chablis. "I think the fish would have gone remarkably well with this," said Askew. Then came a smooth Beaune, with which we had to imagine the duck; and a bottle of Asti Spumante Askew always liked to have with the sweet course. There wasn't any cheese or coffee, but we had the port and brandy just the same and by the end I felt absolutely bloated, although I hadn't had a bite to eat.

What makes a party 'go'? It's something indefinable and as I have emphasised it is nothing to do with being a lavish host. It's easier to say what spoils a party. Top-of-the-list comes the maudlin-man-with-a-chip-on-his-shoulder. He is usually having trouble with his wife, or else she is having trouble with him. Either way, the world is against him.

The best way to deal with people of that sort, or indeed anyone with a grievance, is to appoint an Official Shoulder and an Official Bosom (one man, one woman). They must understand that their sole task at the party is to sympathise heavily with the man who starts saying things like, "We've gotta face it, I just loathe my wife . . ." (Uncle Walter has just peered over my shoulder and commented: "That seems a most reasonable and logical statement for a man to make, my boy".)

Despite what Uncle Walter says, the Official Shoulder and Bosom should be provided with a Sympathy Room to which the Moaner can be removed and encouraged to whine away to his heart's content. This will mean misery for the sympathisers, but may well save the evening as far as the other 20 guests are concerned. The Moaner and his wife should be kept apart, as otherwise they will begin to abuse each other.

I apologise for introducing a note of sadness, but parties can bring out the worst as well as the best in people. Not that Uncle Walter holds marital splits to be sad things.

"My boy," he has just said, "whenever I see a young married couple fighting there is a song in my heart. I feel there is still hope for the poor sod if he can only keep his courage."

Although the task of being a party Shoulder or Bosom may seem rather hard work, it has its rewards. Only the Sympathisers will be in the position next day to disclose (in confidence, of course) the real reason why Juliet and Charles are going to break up as soon as the kids have finished school . . .

So far I have dealt mainly with various forms of the Posh Nosh but the majority of parties are much simpler, of course. The basic type is best described as the Earl's Court Bang, or the Holland Park Thrash. In other words, how Young London spends Saturday nights. I say young London, but the guests may include plenty of 40-year-olds.

I always feel that parties of this sort are for the Coarse Drinker, since they have an air of honesty about them. The rules are quite simple: If you want drink, you've got to bring it; if you want food you've usually got to bring it;

the host however, will provide music, probably a few girls and a floor to sleep on.

One of the drawbacks of the Earl's Court Bang is that the music is usually so loud it not only makes conversation impossible at the party, but makes sleep impossible for three miles around. Which is why this type tends to belong to the young, who appear impervious to noise. However, it is perfectly possible to hold a party with all the good attributes of the Holland Park Thrash—informality, cheapness, and friendliness—without deafening the entire neighbourhood.

A penalty of the informal party is that gatecrashers may try to come in. If these are not welcome, employ the two biggest bores as gatemen or chuckers-out. Some hosts say that the most aggressive people in the party should be appointed but I don't agree. They have a knack of getting involved in trouble, and if they don't find it they look for it.

Like Slasher Williams at the rugby club. Slasher was one of those players who is always getting sent off. In fact several of our opponents had threatened to cancel fixtures if we kept playing him, only we were always so short of men he kept finding himself a game. We usually went to someone's flat for a party on Saturdays and Slasher was always appointed as doorkeeper to stop gatecrashers.

This kept him out of harm's way (his conversation was somewhat moronic, like his rugby) and made him happy. Unfortunately, his piece of tiny power went to Slasher's head. After a time, he started ejecting even people who had received invitations. Pretty girls, who had been specially asked to come along, would be told they couldn't come in.

Eventually, complete megalomania took over, and Slasher began to roam Earl's Court at midnight, going up to total strangers and warning them not to even think of trying to get into the party.

"Excuse me," he'd say, "but were you thinking of going to that smashing party in Bramham Gardens?"

"No," they'd reply. "We didn't even know there was a party there."

"Well, just don't go, that's all," Slasher would warn. "I don't care if you haven't even heard of it, just don't try to get in. You gatecrashers are a menace."

His end came when he refused to admit one of the hosts, on the ground he didn't recognise him, and Slasher himself was banned. Slasher got his revenge the following week by going into the street, collecting a whole mob of strangers, most of them Australians who'd just come off the last District Line train, and marching into the party with them.

I don't know if you've ever been to a party at which an entire coach from the last District Line train arrives, but it does have a tendency to break things up a little.

One of the dangers of holding a good-old-bash in rented flats and rooms is that the first party is often the last, if the landlord is on the premises. For many bachelor boy and girls the housewarming celebration is also the farewell party. Indeed, in my youth, I remember receiving my notice from a Birmingham landlady in the middle of a party and I must say I don't blame her. Someone had upset a bottle of red wine on the floor, we'd not noticed, and a great red stain was spreading all over her ceiling. She originally came up because she thought someone had been stabbed.

I am not going to blame someone who throws out a tenant for a noisy party. People are just as entitled to sleep as they are to have a party. But the Great Coarse Rule to avoid being thrown out is quite simple: Always invite your landlord. People sometimes get ejected because the landlord feels jealous at their having such a good time without him. At least you can avoid that happening. Of course one has to take the risk of the landlord going round acting as a sort of censor of morals, or telling people not to sit on a chair like that, don't they know it cost ten pound just to have it repaired last month?

Beware, also, of the Don Juan property-owner. When I shared a flat in Birmingham the landlord came to a party and vanished with my flat-mate's girl friend. We never saw her again. My friend used to drop strong hints when he paid the rent about, "Have you seen Judy lately?" and all he got was a stony stare. Three months later we were mysteriously evicted *because the landlord was getting married.*

I lost the best billet I ever had in the Army through a party. After years of pigging it as a trooper I'd transferred to the Education Corps, received instant promotion to sergeant, and been posted to an Education Centre ·in Germany. Since in those days Germany was still occupied enemy territory I was rather surprised on arrival to find the centre being run by a former U-Boat Commander. His name was Otto, and such was the force of his personality that I actually saluted him. Apparently, there hadn't been any British at the centre since the last sergeant left three weeks previously and Otto, who was employed as a clerk, had been doing all the teaching, including lectures on such democratic British institutions as the Houses of Parliament.

The education centre was in a vast 19th century house and Otto showed me my room, a great expanse at the top which looked as if it had been furnished by Kaiser Wilhelm II and for which he actually had the cheek to charge me rent. I soon discovered that Otto's rent was really protection money. Next week an officer was posted to us and Otto found him hideous accommodation in the basement. He also doubled the rent of my luxury flat, padlocked the door and told the officer no one had the key, while I pretended to live in barracks.

Of course, it couldn't go on. I made the mistake of holding a party for some sergeant friends with the result that about one a.m. there was the noise of someone beating on the locked door with the butt-end of a revolver, and there was Lieut. Bird shouting, "I'll give you ten seconds to open this door and then I'll shoot!" The guests (and the host) hastily fled through the window and across the roof while Lieut. Bird burst into an empty room.

Next morning he called me in and said excitedly, "Sergeant, I've just discovered a nest of deserters have been living up in that empty attic. I frightened 'em off last night but they left a lot of stuff behind." He indicated my pathetic belongings in a heap behind him. "Just ask Otto to collect this rubbish and burn it will you?"

As Otto said, as he solemnly stuffed my spare uniform into the incinerator, "This wouldn't have happened if you hadn't held that stupid party. I am ashamed of you Sergeant Green."

An interesting variation on the normal party is the Coarse Job Jag or the Working Party. This is most useful when something needs doing about the house. I tend to leave domestic maintenance until the last minute, for instance waiting until the wild gooseberry bushes are coming through the windows, before tackling the garden.

So when a big job needs doing I warn a select body of trusted friends and invite them to a Job Jag, usually on a Sunday morning. Work goes on from 11 to 1.30 at which time endless supplies of cold meat, pickles and drink are dished out. Despite the shortness of the working-time, much is achieved. Twelve guests, each working $2\frac{1}{2}$ hours equals 30 man-hours, which is equivalent to one man working by himself for almost a week.

All is not quite so simple as it looks, however. To start with, abandon hope of any work being done after lunch. The host must also be prepared to have guests in filthy overalls sprawling asleep all over the floor. A firm hand is needed to control guests in their work, otherwise you may find someone pulling up all the radishes in mistake for weeds.

There was a time when I used to dish out drinks immediately the guests arrived, and then give them some more when they had finished, but this had to be abandoned. Few of the guests ever started work, and after three or four drinks most of them were not really capable anyway. Some even went home.

The last straw was when Askew brought half the cricket club along. After drinking an entire barrel of beer between them they went upstairs to do some decorating while I worked in the garden. One can imagine my horror when I looked up from the lawn and saw that someone was *painting over the bedroom window*. I went upstairs and found that the club lunatic had painted every single upstairs window black. It was like a tomb.

In explanation he said, "Well, it'll save you bothering with net curtains. You'll have complete privacy." Fool. If he hadn't have been bigger than me I'd have rammed the paint brush down his throat. As for the rest of the cricket team, two were asleep on my bed, two more were playing cards and another was hopping round the landing trying to get his foot out of a large tin of paint.

It was a lesson I never forgot. Don't issue the drink until the work has been done.

# Travel and Drinking Abroad

*Now spurs the lated traveller apace*
*To gain the timely inn.*

SHAKESPEARE

Travelling is a time of crisis for Coarse Drinkers. They are men of habit and a journey can mean the loss of comfortable, well-established routines. One doesn't realise how much the evening whisky means, while waiting at Charing Cross, until you can't get it.

Not all travel means discomfort, of course. I am a great believer in the pleasures of drinking on trains and ships. In Britain we are well-served by the railways who sell good quality canned beer, useful measures of spirits in small sealed bottles, and reasonable wine. A traveller drinks as well on a British train as on a French, although the food may be inferior (except for afternoon tea, a meal the French have still not mastered).

I always feel grateful to the railways for inventing counter service for drinks, thus establishing the chief feature of the modern bar. Until the railways found in the last century that they needed a method of quick service which the bar provided, drinkers for hundreds of years had had their glasses filled by waiters or drawers, with all the delay that entailed.

Unfortunately, drinking on airlines has become a nightmare. In these days of fast aircraft it has become almost impossible to attract the attention of the steward or stewardess if travelling less than 1,500 miles. By the time the plane has stopped pointing vertically upwards the sweating crew are desperately pushing round those awful plastic meals, and after that there's just time to flog as many duty-free bottles and smokes as they can before service ceases, the plane starts to point vertically downwards and it's all over.

They don't even have time these days to bother with passengers taken ill. I remember sitting next to an unfortunate German on the way to Munich who suddenly let out a great yelp, clutched his chest, and just managed to press the bell for the stewardess before sinking into his seat, groaning. Well, he groaned on for five minutes and nobody came. Then just when I thought he'd expire a stewardess arrived carrying some coffee and said, "Black or white?"

It's lucky it was only indigestion. Although as the girl explained, "If it *was* a heart attack we couldn't do anything could we?"

It seems incredible that once they served a champagne lunch on the Air France Paris flight, and stewardesses (or hostesses as they were known then) were looked on as having a romantic job.

On a longer flight, pressing the button will bring along a girl wearing one of the cold, blank, jet-age expressions that all female cabin staff seem to acquire, and you may ask for a drink. But don't expect any choice of brand or quality. Yet one has to sympathise with the crew. They are the new slaves, servants of a technology which doesn't even allow time to drink.

What a contrast with the good old-fashioned coach outing. Here is where the Coarse Drinker is in his element, with crates of beer on the back seat, pubs flashing by every few minutes and the lads from the social/angling/rugby/cricket/ darts club around him.

But coach trips have their disadvantages, and the Coarse Drinker must beware of them. One is the surly driver in a hurry to get home who refuses to stop anywhere. The most important person on any coach trip is the driver. Do not hesitate to bribe him generously to carry out your wishes. If possible, negotiate beforehand for a driver of known sociable tendencies.

But not *too* sociable. I was on a trip where the driver eloped with a girl passenger and we all had to catch a train back home at midnight.

Almost as big a menace is the know-all driver who insists on stopping at a pub which he recommends. This inevitably turns out to have one crippled barman to serve fifty passengers. Argument is useless, but this sort are sometimes amenable to bribery. Ostentatiously take a collection for the driver and tell him you'd prefer to halt somewhere further on, when you will hand him the money.

Carefully count all members of a coach party before setting out. It is disastrous to return one short, and even more disastrous to return with one too many, or even half-a-dozen too many if another party have got on the wrong coach.

Because of the hazards of drinking while travelling, one cannot emphasise too strongly the value of having a complete Coarse Drinking travel outfit. And by that, I do not mean one of those silly little pocket flasks which hold two ounces of the precious fluid.

Uncle Walter's travelling flask, for instance, holds almost a bottle of whisky (to be precise, $17\frac{2}{3}$ fluid ounces). Indeed, watching Uncle Walter pack for a journey is like seeing someone prepare a mobile bar. His most magnificent preparations used to come when he visited an old friend who was a non-conformist minister, and a strict teetotaller.

It may seem strange that Uncle Walter should be such a close friend of one who did not drink. I used to say as much and Uncle Walter would reply, "My boy, never criticise a man's religion, his moral principles or his garden." I believe they had been childhood friends, but as Uncle said, "Fate sent us our separate ways. He was called to the pulpit; me to the public-bar."

Upon leaving for his annual weekend there, Uncle Walter would remark to my aunt, "It is a dry shop there, Mother," as he prepared himself for the visit. His preparations consisted of an enormous whisky flask, a box of cigars, a lemon, some sugar lumps and small spirit stove (for his nightly toddy); a miniature of gin and one bottle of tonic

*Putting smoke up the chimney*

as a concession to my aunt; and a scent spray. The latter
was to kill the smell of both cigars and alcohol, since the
good minister detested both equally.

On one visit Walter forgot the spray and was reduced to
lying on some cushions on the bedroom floor and puffing
smoke up the chimney. This worked admirably until a
great gobbet of soot fell on his face.

For many years this strange friendship continued, with
Walter not only reduced to smoking and drinking in secret
but forced to attend Public Worship on Sundays. This was a
great sacrifice for a man whose boast had always been
the traditional saying, "The first time I went to church they
threw water over me, the second time confetti, and the next
time it'll be earth."

Unfortunately, it was impossible for Walter to return the
hospitality. His house was full, not so much of drink (although
there was plenty of that) but of all the apparatus associated
with it, such as built-in bars, cocktail cabinets, tantaluses,
soda-siphons, racks, crates, and decanters. Even the dining-
room mirror came from an old country pub in Leicestershire, and bore the legend: "Twice the Man on
Worthington."

In addition, drink keeps popping up in unexpected places at Uncle Walter's. On opening a cupboard in the bedroom where a chamber-pot would normally be kept, one finds a bottle of brandy. My Aunt Gladys is very long-suffering although she once lost patience when she discovered a bottle of Grande Marnier in her sewing-basket. Uncle had hid it there from his brother-in-law whom he believes goes sniffing round the house smelling out the best drinks. As he wanted to preserve the bottle he had secreted it. Whenever his brother-in-law calls Walter rushes about the home, packing away his alcoholic treasures before letting him in.

Walter feared all this would upset his clerical friend, and since he was not prepared to strip the house of almost all its furniture, he was unable to invite him. Yet this strange alliance lasted until the minister died.

"And if he had only drunk a pint of Bass every day," said Uncle Walter sadly after the funeral, "he would not have been called untimely to that Great Resident's Lounge in the sky." I thought this was rather a tactless thing to say about a teetotaller, but Uncle meant well.

One of the dangers of travel is that a Coarse Drinker may find himself cut off from his local beer, although this is less likely to happen nowadays, with the amalgamation of so many breweries. While normally against anything tending towards monopoly, I am not sure that the disappearance of certain local beers is such a bad thing. I can think of half-a-dozen of them—foul, brown, revolting mixtures—which have ruined half-a-dozen holidays, poisoning the entire system, apart from their evil taste.

A change of beer comes particularly difficult to those of us who are sensitive enough to have the Burton palate. This is simply a taste for good Burton beer, and once acquired is difficult to shake off.

"Remember, my boy," Uncle Walter used to say, "that you were born 26¾ miles from Messrs. Bass, Radcliffe and Gretton's noble edifice at Burton-on-Trent. Be proud of your native soil." Indeed, I well remember Uncle Walter setting out to measure the distance from the old Bass brewery in his bull-nosed Morris Cowley tourer and puzzling for years as to why it was a mile longer going than coming back.

Uncle Walter was something of a beer snob and tended to look down on people who were not born in the right area. "The man is positively illegitimate," he would say. "He was born 195 miles from Burton. How can he know anything about beer?"

## Drinking Abroad

In 1945 I was in a military hospital in Italy next to a repulsive soldier suffering from V.D. I hasten to state that *I* was not suffering from that distressing malady. I had suspected pneumonia, but the Army regarded everyone who reported sick as having committed some sort of crime and tended to lump them all together.

Despite my effort to keep as far away from him as possible (can a V.D. germ jump six feet, I kept asking myself, and getting the answer Why not?) we got talking and the subject turned to drink.

"There's only one rule, mate," said my pox-ridden friend. "And that's to drink what the locals drink. If yer in Italy drink what the Wops drink. If yer in China drink what the Chinks drink. It stands to reason, it must be what's best for the area, dunnit?" With which he drained a lemonade bottle full of cheap Chianti.

I remember that man, not merely because he was suddenly arrested at 2 a.m. in his bed, and never seen again, but because his advice was absolutely sound. Half the stomach upsets which people suffer on going abroad are caused not so much by local food and drink, but by a refusal to get accustomed to them gradually, with the result that just a sip of something is enough to lay the traveller low.

The local drink *must* be right for the district, it's the result of thousands of years of experiment. Arrack is refreshing and that's why it's drunk in the Middle East. But it wouldn't go down well on a ski run, any more than ginger wine would on a hot day in Morocco. Even the much-criticised British beer seems to suit our climate and temperament. It goes with a good coal fire, and if tastes in beer are changing perhaps it is due to the disappearance of the traditional open fire.

In general, a good piece of advice when dubious about a local drink abroad is this:

### WHEN IN DOUBT LIGHT IT

Pour some on a saucer and put a match to it. If it doesn't actually explode it can't really do much damage. If it burns with a slow, steady, blue flame, drink with care and moderation. If it goes off bang, throw it away.

(Askew says no, don't throw it away, buy a bottle and bring it home and give it to the person you hate most.)

I shall not attempt anything in the nature of a comprehensive description of drinking customs round the world for the simple reason that I am not qualified to do so. But here are a few random thoughts about various countries which may prove valuable to a Coarse Drinker.

### *Australia*

The Australians are one of the few nations who boast about being drunkards. Other nationalities such as the French may be bigger alcoholics, but they try to hide it. The Australians make no bones about the fact that every male is expected to wallow in beer if he's to prove he is a man.

The success of most social events in Australia is judged purely by the amount of booze drunk (chiefly Australian beer) and has nothing to do with whether everybody enjoyed themselves.

"It were a good wedding," said my dentist reflectively, discussing a function back home in Sydney. "When they came to clear up next morning there was a pile of Foster's lager cans ten feet high in the garden."

Yet he couldn't remember one other detail about the wedding, except that "some joker passed out in the swimming-pool after drinking fifteen cans."

Nothing typifies the Australian attitude to drink better than the experience of a friend who was driving through the outback when he unexpectedly came upon a signpost saying Hotel, pointing up a track. He turned off the main road and after a mile came to a typical Australian bush hotel. His tongue was hanging out by now at the thought of the ice-cold lager but to his dismay he found the place locked, bolted, and shuttered. He kept banging and shouting and after a quarter-of-an-hour an old man's face appeared from an upstairs window and told him to go away.

"It ain't a hotel no more," he shouted. "Me and the old woman won the state lottery last month and we bought this place so we could drink ourselves stupid in peace. And we don't want no jokers like you banging on the doors and disturbing us."

Although nearly unconscious through thirst by now, my friend says he could not help admiring the old man.

## New Zealand

The New Zealand attitude to drink is influenced by the peculiar licensing laws of the country and the puritan influence, which tend to make all public drinking a sin.

All this has made the New Zealanders a nation of home brewers. Your average Kiwi can't look at a bath without measuring its capacity and sizing it up for use as a vat in connection with some home-made beer.

I once shared a flat in London with three New Zealand lads from my rugby team. I think I can swear that in six months I never once managed to get a bath there, because the damn tub was full of some alcoholic mixture fermenting. You couldn't even sleep, because it kept making bubbling noises in the night. Meanwhile, bottles of home-made wine would be going off like machine guns. At intervals of a fortnight the mixture in the bath would be siphoned off and drunk in vast orgies that went on for days and finished with the flat being strewn with unconscious people.

Every time they held a party I hoped I'd get a chance to clean out the bath and have a quick wash, but I always succumbed to the home-made brew before I could get to the bath. Ironically enough, the nearest I came to having a bath was when I had to sleep there after a party, my own bed being occupied by three guests.

## Ireland

Thanks to the delightful system whereby every grocer's shop is a pub, it is positively dangerous to buy a tin of corned beef in the country districts of Ireland. I went on a walking holiday over there once. It must have been the shortest walking tour ever taken. We never carried on past eleven o'clock in the morning, when we would go into a grocery shop for some baked beans or bacon. "It's a soft morning, then" the man would say and we'd agree, and he'd say you'd better have some Guinness and we'd agree, and the next thing we knew we'd be saying goodbye at two o'clock in the morning.

The only time I was nearly disappointed was one Sunday when we knocked on a shop and they wouldn't open and we stood outside in the rain wondering what to do. Suddenly there was a great noise and a jaunty car full of middle-aged women waving umbrellas and shouting pulled up. The door opened, they vanished inside and it closed. Now the law says that if you're *bona fide* travellers you can have a drink so we knocked and knocked but nobody came and we had to stand in the rain again until bless my soul, *another* jaunty car full of shouting women came galloping up. This time we got our foot in the door and asked to come in.

"We're shut lads," said the owner. "It's Sunday."

"But we've come from Whitestown," we protested.

His face broke into a huge grin. "Ah, well now, why didn't ye tell me ye was *bonas fides*?" he shouted. "Come on in."

Such pleasant experiences are aided by the flexibility of the Irish police in their attitude to licensing hours. The only time I ever knew them to interfere was in the back parlour of a grocer's shop near Wexford about one a.m., when a policeman burst in.

"Do you mind drinking up and leaving," he demanded. "We're raiding this bar in half-an-hour."

But beware the Great Irish Myth that all the Dublin bars are full of poets and playwrights and all the country bars full of witty peasants. Ireland has more bores per thousand of the population than anywhere else in the world. Or perhaps it's just that being Irish, the bores are more talkative.

One thing which distinguishes them is their immense ignorance of Ireland. In an effort to break a monologue lasting 25 minutes I once asked an Irish pub bore what he thought of Brendan Behan.

"Who did he play for?" he asked.

Sometimes, in country districts, the bore may even burst into a whining dirge which he alleges is a traditional Irish song and for this may expect a drink.

For years I used to wonder how a pleasant people like the Irish could stand their peculiar brand of bore until I sought escape from one in Guinness and found that if I drank enough I didn't care. I think the secret of Ireland is that the whole nation is permanently and happily sozzled. I should have realised this years ago from playing rugby against the Irish. That strange stench of stout in the scrum at ten a.m. could only come from men who were pickled in the stuff.

## Scotland

I always find it difficult to understand why the average Scot is such a heavy drinker since he rarely seems to get any enjoyment out of the stuff. Perhaps it's a hangover from the strict Calvanist tradition but to so many Scotsmen drinking is not a pleasure, it's a grim rite of getting plastered as quickly as possible. They say the quickest way out of Manchester is a bottle of whisky and the same may be true of Glasgow.

I once sat in a Glasgow pub and watched four men having the Scottish idea of a perfect Saturday night. They walked in and ordered four halves of beer and four double Scotches. Then they repeated this eight times. They said little but drank in silence. At closing time they all walked out and fell over. They helped each other up and weaved away down the street and another Saturday night had passed.

The Scottish attitude to drinking is shown by their pubs, which from the outside resemble public conveniences which have been half-wrecked by vandals. Inside they are little better, with no concessions to civilised amenities such as carpets or even chairs. Not that the drinkers would notice—they're too busy standing at the bar and pouring it down.

Scottish hotels are more civilised, although the designation "hotel" is more often than not a way of circumventing the restrictions on Sunday drinking. Yet the old puritan tradition still remains and I know one Scottish hotel where the text "Remember the Sabbath Day to Keep it Holy" looms menacingly over the entrance to the bar where the Sunday drinkers are pouring in.

Incidentally, remember that on Saturday nights all men in Glasgow under 5 ft 6 in. high (and there are thousands of them) seek fights with people bigger than themselves. Since they will readily invent an excuse if they haven't got one, the simplest thing to do if approached is to say, "Hit me now Jock and get it over."

## Wales

The Welsh attitude to drink is ambivalent. As a nation they probably have more nominal teetotallers than any in Europe yet the per capita consumption of beer is probably the highest, and most of it is consumed outside of licensing hours. In fact this is a Welsh peculiarity, that they enjoy a drink best when it's illegal. A Welshman will drink quite normally during permitted hours but the minute drinking becomes illegal his eyes glisten and he starts to drink twice as fast. Which is why on Sunday afternoons Wales is one vast illegal drinking club. Not to mention those parts of England where Welsh circles predominate.

Unlike other races, the Welsh still manage to sing quite tunefully after a few drinks. Hence the tale of the group of Welshmen who hired a minibus for an outing. On the way back one of them tried to lead the singing but was shouted down.

"You're too drunk to sing," said the organiser. "If you can't do better than that you'll have to drive."

## Egypt

A Coarse Drinker must remember that some North African and Middle-East countries are not drink-orientated. By that I don't mean they are teetotal, but they don't gear their lives to booze as do we Europeans.

Twice I have been to excellent receptions in Egypt—one by the Governor of Luxor and the other by students of Alexandria University. Each was the sort of occasion which in Europe would have called for great vats of gin. One may

*The high spot of each reception*

therefore imagine my feelings when I had to sustain myself
on tea and cakes (just try talking politics for four hours on
tea and cakes). The high spot of each reception was a
belly-dance. I never thought I should live to see the day
when I watched a belly-dance from behind a teapot while
eating jam tarts. So be prepared to fit in with local custom
and remember the Coarse Drinker's travelling rule: A
bottle in the bedroom is worth two at the table.

## Birmingham

The inclusion of Birmingham in a section on drinking abroad
is not a mistake, simply an indication of how I feel about the
place. Birmingham may well have changed these days but in
the early fifties I was actually rebuked by a policeman for
whistling a tune in the street. It is typical of the old Birmingham that they served a measure of beer I have never seen
elsewhere. It was called a Stick, and was one-third of a
pint. It was drunk largely by that peculiar breed of Birmingham charwomen and they had the incredible knack of
making a stick of mild ale last for two hours. And that was
their night out.

## America

Anyone drinking with Americans must remember they are
totally incapable of drinking in moderation. The quiet
half-pint is as unknown in America as the small automobile.
Assume, therefore, if invited to any function involving drink
by an American that the place will be swimming in the hard
stuff. Beer is not really considered alcoholic, which is hardly
surprising since it's so highly-chilled as to have all alcohol
and flavour driven out.

Americans are also afraid of drinks in their pure form.
Be prepared for continual attempts to adulterate liquor by
adding something or turning it into a cocktail. Even Scotch
will have ice in it.

Small measures are unknown. As the Americans are very
generous hosts one's glass is permanently full and hosts are

constantly urging guests to drink a little so they can put some more in. To avoid giving offence, I keep hiding my glass at American parties, with the result there is a trail of half-empty Scotch glasses round the room. They must find them afterwards in every nook and cranny—stuffed down the grand piano, behind the radiators, on the window sills, even inside vases. Even then I'm awash in 30 minutes.

This habit once got me into trouble. I used to be invited regularly to the house of some American friends employed at the London Embassy, and one day the wife rang me up in great distress.

"Mike," she said, "you know all about indoor plants and things don't you?"

Well, I didn't, but on the strength of having kept a rubber plant alive for a year I had some reputation so I said yes, and she continued, "Well I wish you'd come over and look at my plants. They've all suddenly died."

I must say she hadn't exaggerated. Entering her house was like looking at a Goya painting of a massacre. All these little plants were sprawled all over their pots in contorted positions as if they had died in agony, and some of them had gone black.

I then realised what had happened. For six months I'd been pouring those vast American Scotches she served into the flower-pots and those poor little plants had been poisoned by whisky. Fortunately I had the wit to say, "It looks like Fuller's disease to me. You'll have to change the soil and start again."

This left me with the problem of where to dispose of my unwanted drinks in future (she immediately thanked me by giving me a Scotch big enough for six). For several parties after that I was reduced to all sorts of devices like slinking out of the room with my glass and tipping the surplus out of the window. Even that led to trouble because a neighbour told my host. "That must have been some party you had yesterday. Scotch was pouring out of the windows and dripping down the walls . . ."

Beware also of the weird "genuine American" drinks which appear at U.S. parties. I mean strangely-shaped bottles of

6

yellow liquid with a title like "C'nel Cornseed's Old Kentucky Acorn Brandy—345 degrees proof". The label will bear a picture of some male model dressed to represent a Southern Gentleman leering at the prospective customer and holding up a glass. The label will also have some palpable lie like, "As served to Confederate troops before the battle of Gettysburg." No wonder they lost.

No self-respecting American ever drinks this sort of stuff—they stick to Scotch. But they put it out at parties in case the guests would like it, rather as we might put out a bottle of mead or beetroot wine.

Considering the enthusiasm with which they fill you up before a meal, it is rather surprising to find that Americans drink little with their food except iced water. I once carried my gigantic Scotch to the table at one U.S. meal, on the grounds that even Scotch was better than water.

"Mr. Green," cried my hostess. "You can't drink Scotch with smoked salmon."

No, I thought, I couldn't. What a good woman. Bring out the hock.

She went away and came back with a bottle of Coke. I don't know if you've ever had smoked salmon and Coke but I don't recommend it. The only consolation was that as with all American meals, I was so dazed with booze by the time I sat down I hardly knew what I was eating anyway.

The American dislike of half-measures is carried into their bars too. Drinking in an American bar is punctuated by the sound of people sliding from their stool to the floor. Nobody seems to take any notice. This can make conversation a trifle difficult. Americans are always extremely anxious to start up a conversation but half the people in a bar will be capable of little else other than insane gibberish that sounds like "Awllll—bubble—birllll—yourble—yeah?"

If you just say "Yeah" back they seem quite happy.

*Sweden*

Sweden needs mentioning because of the peculiar national attitude to drink about which intending travellers must be warned. The Swedes, officially at any rate, frown on drink. They make it expensive to get enough of it. Oddly enough, their attitude to drink is rather like that of the Victorian English to sex, which was publicly unmentionable but which flourished furtively. While the Swedish attitude to sex is rather like the Victorian attitude to booze—they saw nothing wrong in the pubs being open all day.

Take a Swedish girl out for the evening and she'll probably ask, "Do you wish to make love to me tonight? Because if so, I must put the cat out early."

But ask her to have more than one drink and she becomes terribly coy, rather as if a shocking suggestion has been made, and says, "Oh you naughty man, you want to get me drunk don't you? I have heard of you English . . ."

The result is that the Swedes rush to such places as Denmark and Spain for their drink rather as the Victorian English used to rush to Paris for their sex. Not that the poor Swedes seem to get much pleasure out of either vice. They bring such a gloomy, mechanistic approach, that all the fun is lost. No wonder they have the highest suicide rate in Europe.

*Greece*

I mention Greece because as far as I know it is the only country in Europe where you can buy ginger-beer. They sell it on the island of Corfu under its Greek name of Tsin-tsin beer. Ginger beer is a relic of the English occupation of the island 150 years ago. Apart from the ruins of a fort the other thing the English left behind is cricket. There are three local sides, who play on a matting wicket on the main square of the island's capital and the annual Corfu Cricket Week, when teams come over from England, is famous.

I once had the pleasure of taking part in the Cricket Week with a team from Kent appropriately called the Imbibers, and I feel the English game could learn a lot from the Greeks,

To start with, the entire ground (which, as I said, consists of the main square) is surrounded by café tables at which waiters are serving drinks. Tsin-tsin beer and ouzo is an interesting combination while waiting to bat or even when fielding. Indeed, Corfu is one of the few cricket grounds in the world where it is possible to order a drink while fielding at square-leg and have it gravely brought to you by a white-coated waiter with the change on a plate.

This may account for the poor performance often put up by visiting sides. For instance, in one of the Imbiber's games, almost the entire on-side field were overcome by temptation and sneaked off to a table. This was only discovered when a ball was hit high and straight to square leg on the boundary. It was then discovered there was no square-leg, and no fine-leg and no mid-wicket either. They had taken over a table near the boundary where their position was revealed by the sound of "The One-Eyed Riley" being sung at the tops of their voices. And all this at eleven o'clock in the morning . . . No wonder we lost by 50 runs.

# 7 Drinking and Indoor Sports

*It was remarked to me by the late Mr Charles Roupell . . . that to play billiards well was a sign of an ill-spent youth.*

HERBERT SPENCER

Some hobbies and pastimes are so inextricably tied up with drinking that it is impossible to imagine them apart. Darts, for instance. How can anybody play darts over a cup of coffee? In fact the game isn't the same played outside a pub, any more than shove ha'penny is. I couldn't possibly stand all evening in someone's dining-room throwing darts, but I'd cheerfully do it in a public-bar.

True to their philosophy of giving priority to drink, Coarse Drinkers will naturally seek those hobbies where drink can not only be consumed, but where it is an integral part of the whole proceeding. I have already referred to the inseperable links between darts and beer (you can't play darts properly on gin-and-tonic), but there are other hobbies where drink can be closely linked with the game itself, and some of them may seem rather unexpected choices.

For instance, if asked at which sport I have imbibed most freely, it might surprise many to hear the answer: Chess. This is quite true. In no other indoor game does drink play so great a part with me. Provided one's partner is like-minded, a few drinks make for some extraordinary games. As the match develops, and a few whiskies get under the belt, the whole secret of chess becomes crystal clear. Knights, bishops, pawns form fantastic patterns. The way to a check-mate is so obvious. Incredible moves are invented, such as

*Games of this type are mercifully short*

Green's Gambit (sacrificing every piece you've got for the opponent's Queen).

Games of this type are mercifully short, as are all the best chess games. Should a contest drag on, however, the end-game is liable to be somewhat bizarre. I shall always remember being discovered about midnight using a pepper-pot as a rook. At this stage the rules are liable to be bent a little. Players will move pieces in vast circles; pawns sweep in great parabolas. The game is won by the man who stays awake the longest.

Another indoor hobby admirably suited for a Coarse Drinker is amateur dramatics. The *camaradie* of the theatrical dressing-room can be as enjoyable as that of the sports pavilion, although some producers and directors would take a more serious view.

They are probably worried, and rightly too, by the many legends of the Stage Drunk, although most of the stories are about professionals. The most legendary Stage Drunk was the old ham who was tight when he made his first entrance as Richard III. After tripping up as he came on, he made three efforts to say the first line and got it wrong each time. A voice from the gallery shouted, "You're drunk."

"If you think I'm drunk," retorted the aged actor with

great dignity, "just wait until you see the Duke of Buckingham!"

It is typical of the topsy-turvy world of the stage that while drinking in the dressing-room is great fun, drinking on stage presents enormous difficulties.

One of the strangest things about it is the tradition that instant jollity can be aroused simply by saying some idiotic line like, "But come my jolly lads, let us drink to the sweethearts we have left behind us." At which all the actors wave empty mugs in the air and give a great shout of merriment before bursting into song. (Has anyone ever tried the experiment of going into a public-bar and saying, "But come my jolly lads etc. etc." and seeing what *really* happens? I should be interested to know. I also query whether people really do wave their mugs in the air. I should think it would spill the beer).

However, since a Coarse Drinker may well be a Coarse Actor too, in an amateur company he is likely to find himself with one of those moronic little roles as part of a roistering crew of jolly fellows.

Unless the actor takes positive steps himself, he will inevitably find he has an empty mug on stage. It is wise, therefore, to raise a collection and bribe an assistant stage-manager to have the actor's mugs filled with beer. This will give some stimulation while listening to the hero singing *Overhead the Moon is Beaming*.

Do not wave the mugs too vigorously, and I write as one who has seen the Merry Widow receive a tankard full of ale right in her kisser. Remember also, to ensure that they are the real thing. I shall not forget a performance of Henry IV (Part Two) being ruined when all the papier maché mugs got soggy and fell apart.

Finally, make sure the mugs contain something drinkable. It is difficult to look cheerful after some idiot has filled them all with cold gravy and the entire cast, having toasted the herione generously, are now looking for somewhere to vomit.

One of my most alarming experiences came because I forgot my own rule of always sniffing any stage drink to make sure it's potable. It was a scene in which I was supposed to come into a room, read a letter which gave me a terrible shock, pour a glass of water with trembling hands and drain it at one gulp.

Unfortunately, the property-girl filled the water carafe from a plain bottle which the stage manager always kept on his desk and which she foolishly assumed was water. It was not. It was his secret supply of gin, deliberately kept in an anonymous container.

Well, I read the letter, started trembling and gasping, poured out the 'water' and swallowed about half-a-pint of neat gin in one gulp. I let out a ghastly shriek, and fled into the wings gasping for real water. It took some time to find it, during which the stage was empty, but apparently the whole thing passed off quite smoothly. The audience thought it was a brilliant piece of acting while the local newspaper positively raved.

"Michael Green's big scene came in the second act," they commented, "when he receives the news that Sheila has deserted him for Jonathan and taken away the child. Until then one may have thought Mr. Green was playing a trifle monotonously, mis-timing some lines and forgetting others altogether. But his big moment compensated for everything. On reading Sheila's farewell letter he gave a positively animal cry of anguish which seemed to come from the very depths of his being and fled, tortured, from the room.

"By a superb trick of production Mr. Green did not return immediately, and the audience were left to contemplate the empty stage for several minutes during which nothing could be heard but the heart-rending sobs of Mr. Green off-stage. Was the empty stage symbolic of the character's empty life? Perhaps. But this critic, for one, found it difficult to repress a tear when Mr. Green returned having apparently aged ten years by grief. At first he could only mouth helplessly and when he did speak it was in a voice hoarse with emotion. Rarely has one seen amateur acting reach such a pitch of intensity."

I have already referred to the fact that small-part actors should provide themselves with a *little* alcohol on the stage.

But I must warn against a lot. I was once in a crowd scene where we had to sit around a pub table, just mumbling and drinking, while terrible events took place in front of us. The idea was to show how life must still go on no matter what has occurred.

Life went on all right, rather too vigorously I'm afraid. It being someone's birthday, he offered to pay for any drinks supplied on stage and we all opted for genuine whisky. Within ten minutes the principal actors were looking nervously over their shoulders at the babble of conversation behind them. Halfway through the scene the extras were trying to start up a song and the final, dramatic climax was completely wrecked when two of them fell off their chairs with laughter.

It was a new play and the author rushed backstage afterwards and complained bitterly to the producer, "Do those drunken idiots realise they are supposed to represent the Life Force?"

For later performances the Life Force were given cold tea instead of whisky. But I am not sure that the play was quite so exhilarating for the audience, even if the author was satisfied.

While on the subject of drink and the amateur stage, I must mention the awful experience of Askew as a warning to Coarse Drinkers never to let their thirst get out of hand.

Askew was playing in a village hall in Surrey. He had an entrance in Act One and another in Act Three with an hour's rest in between, so he used to sneak out of the back of the hall, and cross the churchyard into the village pub and play darts, despite the fact that he was dressed as the Duke of Wellington.

What with the beer and the darts he lost track of time until he glanced at the clock and saw with horror that he was due on stage in two minutes. He fled from the public-bar and dashed across the churchyard, where in the darkness he fell into a newly-dug grave and broke his ankle.

Meanwhile on stage his cue came and went, and there was an embarrassed silence in the hall until in the distance the audience heard a terrible oath and faint, bleating cries for

*"Why don't we just shovel earth on top of him and save everybody a load
of trouble"*

help. The performance was abandoned and they all trooped
out into the churchyard where they found Askew crawling
around in the bottom of the grave, trying to recover his
darts, which had fallen from his pocket.

The producer of the play looked down at Askew and
commented bitterly: "Why don't we just shovel earth on
top of him and save everybody a load of trouble?"

Returning to the subject of pub games, I always feel
playing something makes the beer go down better. It's not
only the actual exercise involved (such as walking to the dartboard), but the contest gives a subject for conversation and
breaks up the static group round a table. It is a poor Coarse
Drinker who cannot play most pub games a little, and one
particularly well.

To me darts will always remain the king of bar games and I like to think that you can still find pubs where one of my better throws has been pencilled on the wall along with the other great feats. Although I must admit that at times I wonder whether darts is entirely suitable as a relaxation in a place where drink is sold.

I wouldn't recommend a game, for instance, at an office leaving party or during a coach stop on the way back from a rugby match. I still recall with horror the sight of an outraged landlord vaulting over the bar with a dart sticking out of his neck and pursuing the frightened thrower down the road. All might yet have been well if the team idiot had not remarked to the landlord, as he returned panting, "I say, old chap, did you know you've got a dart sticking out of your neck?" This time everybody had to leave.

Pub games offer endless opportunities for the Coarse Drinker to indulge in a little Coarse Sport. After all, your opponents will almost certainly be doing the same. For instance, I have never yet played darts in a strange pub where the locals didn't twist the rules to their own advantage. The fact is that in England darts' rules genuinely *do* differ from district to district. In Leicestershire, for instance, the rule on "busting" is different from that in Warwickshire (except for border villages).

A Coarse Drinker is entitled to turn these variations to his own advantage. Opponents may be unsettled by a preliminary dispute over rules. Wherever they stand, object. If they stand at 8 ft 6 in. say, "In this part of the world we play at nine feet." One might also add something confusing like, "Are we playing London or Midland rules?" Having raised some muddle in the minds of the opposition, ostentatiously move well out of the way as they throw their first dart, and cower with the implication that anyone within twenty feet is in mortal peril.

A friend goes so far as to invent imaginary rules such as the use of five darts each, or starting with a treble, but I disagree with this.

The finest darts' wheeze I ever saw was by a young art student who used to chalk nude women all over the scoreboard. The effect was incredible. No matter where one tried to aim a dart it always missed the board and finished up in the naked woman. It would have been worth a study by Freud.

Askew keeps a special set of darts for lending to opponents and this is most effective. Although outwardly normal, they are in fact totally unbalanced and when thrown tend to behave like a drunken boomerang. The points are so blunt they wouldn't stick in a Christmas pudding. However, the borrower usually has two or three unsuccessful shots before he hands them back.

So much injury has been caused to customers by these darts, however, that in at least three pubs Askew has been asked not to use them. But as Askew says, they're no worse than the darts the landlord usually provides.

I firmly believe that *bar billiards* was invented by the Devil. I find the frustration of losing one's complete score through striking the black mushroom completely unbearable, not to mention the nervous tension involved.

However, like darts, it does give an opportunity for the invention of rules. Everyone I play against always seems to make up their own, drivel like, "In this pub old man, every-thing counts triple value after the landlord has called last orders." Personally, I always tell an opponent who hits the ball off the table that under our rules I take all his points.

One would like to advise readers to ensure that their opponent gets a bent cue. Unfortunately, *all* bar billiards' cues are not merely bent, but positively distorted. But try to get hold of the only one with a tip before the opposition do the same.

*Shove ha'penny* is a game where the physical conditions of making the strike are vital. In important matches I am so tense a cough will put me off. I do not suggest one should cough just as an opponent is about to strike, but it might not be a bad idea to take a huge breath as if you were about to sneeze, and hold it.

No man can remain unmoved if out of the corner of his eye he sees that two feet away someone is holding their breath and going red in the face.

I do not agree with such crude methods as dropping ha'pennies in puddles of beer; pretending to clean a dirty ha'penny on a sticky handkerchief; or spilling a pint of beer over the board.

But I see no reason why just before the stroke one should not say, "That *is* your glass is it?" Nothing upsets a man more than a faint suggestion that he has been drinking out of the wrong glass. An alternative is, "What is that floating in the top of your beer?"

*Cribbage* is another game with which every Coarse Drinker should be familiar. Unfortunately, I find the game a cross between conjuring and higher mathematics, and no one will allow me to play with them any longer as I am so painfully slow counting up and pegging my score. It strikes me as a game designed by cheats for cheats. *Dominoes* is about my level. It appears to be cheat-proof, except for blatantly peering at someone else's hand.

It's good to see there are still traditional local bar games played in different parts of the country. West Country pubs still have their skittle alleys (and so do some West Country clubs) while in Northamptonshire their own peculiar form of pub skittles is still popular. This version is played with flat wooden discs called cheeses, and the nine pins are set up on a big leather-covered table with a net at the back. Strangely enough, I don't think this game exists outside of Northants, and the neighbouring areas. It's great fun and immensely popular but one can almost plot the Northamptonshire border by where it's played.

Then there are still a few esoteric old sports, such as Knurr and Spell (I didn't make that up, they play it in Sheffield). The old English game of Stoolball is still played in Sussex pubs and so is marbles. While up in Shropshire and round the Welsh borders you can still play quoits.

A Coarse Drinker does not need to know the rarer sports, but if one wished to make an impression on a snooty hotel manager, one might ask him, "Tell me, where is the Knurr and Spell pitch?"

Alas, the fruit machine has become the most popular amusement in many bars, although I refuse to count it as a

sport. Any device which takes a pound in silver and then
spews out a few miserable counters worth 10p is little better
than a mechanical thief and I only wish I had the self-
control to avoid the wretched things. At least there was just
an element of sport about the manual type of fruit machine,
and one could deceive oneself that there was a certain amount
of skill in the way the handle was pulled. Hence wild legends
that it was possible to turn up the winning line fifteen times in
succession by careful manipulation of the handle. The
fruit machine is part of the decline in the British Way of
Drink.

I wouldn't mention the *drinking contest* except for the fact
that man's history from Roman times onwards shows a long
list of contests involving drink. A Coarse Drinker should
know the different forms they take, but only so he can avoid
them.

A common version is simply the contest to see who can
drink a pint the quickest. These are always won by a certain
type of human Freak—the Man Without a Swallow—so it's
no use ordinary people trying to compete. The Freaks just
open their gullets and pour the stuff down in a few seconds.
Dick Hawkins, a great second-row forward for Northampton
just after the war, had the gift of doing this endlessly and
the team used to set him up against the opposition champions
and lay bets. The only person who never won any money was
poor old Dick—he was too busy pouring it down.

The Boat Race is a variation in which contestants form
relay teams. Each man has to drink half a pint before the next
can move. Both teams always end up drenched in beer.
Another type of contest involves a challenge to have a drink
in every bar in a certain area or street. Avoid such challenges
like the plague—there are always three times as many pubs
as you think. They sprout up everywhere. Cambridge
undergraduates have—or used to have—the King Street
Run in which competitors have to drink a pint in every pub
in King Street in a certain time. There used to be a favourite
challenge in Leicester to drink a pint in every pub within
200 yards of the Clock Tower but when you came to try it
you suddenly found there were two dozen of the wretched

things, furtively lurking up alleys where nobody ever went.

I have to confess that when young and foolish I once took part in a drinking contest myself, in Birmingham of all places. Certain remarks passed between me and a friend which could only be wiped out in mild ale and we duly met at the Cambridge Arms (now demolished, like most of old Birmingham). My opponent began by drinking his initial pint in ten seconds flat while I was still blowing the froth off mine, and then said, "Hurry up—let's have another." This wasn't a very promising start. By seven o'clock he was three pints ahead (six to three). My three spare pints were lined up on the table, all lukewarm and flat, and victory seemed beyond me. In fact I was about to concede the contest when my second, a girl, whispered, "Don't give up Mike, he's turned mauve." I looked and it was true. My opponent had indeed turned a strange hue.

Inspired by the knowledge that he was at least human I kept on. By nine o'clock I was level with my opponent who had gone chalk-white and stopped drinking. At quarter to ten I was well ahead and offered him a draw. He accepted and hastily left the bar.

Which proves that in drinking as in anything else slow and steady wins the race. But drinking contests are young men's folly. The sign of a mature drinker is that he never tries to force it down and doesn't mind leaving a little in the bottom of his glass.

If love-making is considered a branch of indoor sport, then it belongs in this section. But I cannot better that wise old bird Shakespeare's comments in Macbeth, when the porter says that as regards lechery, drink "provokes the desire, but it takes away the performance . . ."

Drink can also provide a fatal mental barrier to success with women. It acts as the Great Deceiver, which is why at any party you will see fine, splendid-looking fellows ignored by girls for sneaky, rat-faced individuals whose only saving grace is that they have remained sober enough to concentrate and not dissipate their attentions.

These are the Six Stages of Deception which drink imposes concerning women:

STAGE ONE: A young man has a couple of drinks and looks forward to meeting a smashing bird at the party.

STAGE TWO: Success! He walked in the room and there she was. Now they're drinking together.

STAGE THREE: He's now finished the bottle of plonk he brought along and is pinching someone else's can of beer. This is where tragedy is about to set in.

STAGE FOUR: Doom. He becomes convinced he can cope with two or three girls at once. "After all," the booze assures him, "are you not the wittiest person on earth? Why not try that other bird by the door? Maybe you will make both!"

STAGE FIVE: The young man is now muttering that women have no sense of humour, personally he thought it was rather funny when he balanced a pint on his head and upset beer all over her dress. But if she wants to be stuck up he'll go back to that original bird, only she seems to have vanished.

STAGE SIX: It is 3 a.m. All the women have gone except for two or three attached girls. Our young man joins the gang of unsuccessful lovers discussing football in the kitchen while his original bird disappears down the stairs with a thing in rainbow jeans on which he has painted an arrow pointing at his loins.

Why Nature should be so perverse I do not know, but it is not those happy spirits who apply themselves to the bottle generously who get the women at parties. It is the three-glasses-of-beer sneaker. So beware of Stage Four, unless you've brought your own girl.

# 8 *Lubricating Outdoor Sports*

*No man is fit to be called a sportsman
wot doesn't kick his wife out of bed on
a haverage once in three weeks!*

R. S. SURTEES (Handley Cross)

Most Coarse Drinkers will probably be Coarse Sportsmen.
It is difficult to see how it could be otherwise, since I once
defined a Coarse Sportsman as: "One who, when his club
receive a grant from the National Playing Fields Association,
wants to spend it on extending the bar."

Any why not? The enjoyment of most outdoor sports
and games is increased immensely by a moderate amount of
alcohol. ("Why moderate?" says Uncle Walter. "This
namby-pamby book of yours will never sell, my boy.")
The old idea was that sport and drinking didn't mix.
Victorian books were full of advice to young sportsmen to
stick to Adam's Ale and to suppress impure thoughts.
Today, anyone who suppresses impure thoughts is considered
a candidate for the psychiatrist, and drinking is viewed by
many to be not only an integral part of sport, but sometimes
the prime objective.

I have never even considered taking part in a sport which
involved giving up drink. Askew goes further and says that if
he has to be completely sober to participate in something
then the game is not worth playing at all. Rather an extreme
viewpoint, although Askew gives it force by adding that any
game he is fit to play must be a pretty rotten sport anyway.

There are a few happy games at which a player can
refresh himself in the middle of the match (such as golf,
tennis and cricket). But usually the proper place for a drink

7

is before and after. To a Coarse Drinker, what could not be tolerated would be a sport where you didn't drink either before or after, such as cross-country running or motor-cycle racing.

Perhaps I am being unfair on cross-countries, only I have a particular fear of them ever since I was chosen for the 4th Armoured Brigade cross-country in the bitter German winter of 1947. I had to withdraw through a fortuitous illness and the man who took my place was carried in with a frostbitten penis. He never forgave me.

Despite what Uncle Walter says, however, one must counsel moderation in the interests of the Coarse Drinker himself. My own experience, for what it is worth, is that over-indulgence either during or before a game brings nothing but disaster, although at the time everything probably seems fine.

As a warning, let me quote what happened to Askew in the tennis club mixed doubles final. Like all Coarse Sportsmen, Askew is secretly and pathetically keen to do well, being prevented from doing so only by his own total incompetence and his refusal to practise.

But this time Askew got to the final, largely because he had a bye in the first round and was carried by his partner in the others. The final was on a Saturday afternoon, and Askew, who was nervous, begged me to meet him for a beer and a sandwich to cheer him up. We met at twelve, and the game was at three. Thus the stage was set for disaster, and it is sufficient to say that when we got to the tennis club we had had the beer but somehow the sandwiches got left out.

Askew's arrival was rather unusual. He danced down the drive shouting, "Bring 'em out! Let 'em all come! I'm ready for 'em!" and swinging his racket in great arcs, as a result of which he struck a post and shattered the racket. Undeterred, he burst into the clubhouse, embraced his partner passionately, made an insulting gesture at his opponents and borrowed another racket.

Upon arriving on court he produced a bottle of rum, took a pull from it, offered it all round and carefully placed it in a corner of the court. He then demanded that some practice balls be sent over. Six were served and he missed the lot.

There was quite a crowd round the court when the umpire called for play to start. Askew, who was receiving, crouched tensely on the baseline, but just as the server threw the ball into the air he called out loudly, "Would you mind waiting a moment old man, I have an urgent appointment in the gents' lavatory," and rushed off to the changing-rooms.

When he returned, he entered the wrong court. Realising his mistake he tried to get out, but by this time he couldn't find the door and was reduced to feeling his way round the netting like someone lost in a dark room. Mercifully, a spectator opened the door just when he had given up and was trying to climb over the netting like a giant spider with his racket in his teeth.

The umpire called for silence and play began again. The first serve was a fault. This was just as well as Askew had his back to the server, exchanging insults with a spectator. The second ball was in court and Askew aimed a savage slash at it. Unfortunately, he not only missed the ball altogether, but the racket flew out of his hand and hit his partner on the head, knocking her unconscious.

To make matters worse, Askew was under the impression that his partner had been knocked senseless by the ball. He kept shouting at the server, "You are no gentleman sir! No gentleman would aim a ball at a lady like that. You are nothing but a tennis-playing skunk, sir, and I demand that you concede the game, set, match, tournament and title!"

He was dragged off the court still babbling and that was the end of the final. Later the whole affair was settled quite simply, if somewhat drastically. Askew was expelled from the club and the trophy awarded to the other couple.

But then my own position in the club became impossible. Every time Askew passed the courts in the road outside, he would press himself against the netting like a chimpanzee and bellow at me, "Call yourself a friend? You ought to be ashamed of yourself playing with those cheats. You know one of them nearly killed a woman with his service?"

In the end I had to resign as well. Yet as so often happens when drink is involved, the truth of the affair cannot be brought home to its chief participant. To his dying day Askew will remain convinced that it was the server who knocked his partner senseless.

The above story should be sufficient warning of the perils of over-indulgence, yet we humans never learn. I must confess to having disgraced myself at cricket. It was a hot day and I was in the outfield near the pavilion. Nobody was trying to hit the ball very hard, so with the help of a friend I refreshed myself with half a pint of beer every alternate over, when I came to that particular position.

The disaster occurred when, after many overs and eight pints, I was asked to bowl. I am not normally requested to do so, since I am one of the few men in the game to have pitched an off-break on the head of the square-leg umpire, but apparently they thought the only way to get out the other side was to tempt them to hit. I certainly do that all right—if the batsmen can get near enough the ball to hit it at all.

Normally I toss up slow tweakers, known to my friends as Vicarage Balls for some reason, but inspired by a gallon of beer I decided this was a time to bowl fast. The captain looked in astonishment as I paced out a 40-yard run. I then re-set the field so that every man was within three yards of the bat and hurtled towards the wicket at about 30 m.p.h. The rest of the team swear that I was shouting threats and insults at the white-faced batsman as I ran up and short-leg cried, "My God, he's going to kill us all!" Unfortunately, the effect was spoiled by the fact that I crashed straight into the stumps at the bowler's end before releasing the ball, causing injury to what Uncle Walter calls one's "marriage equipment".

My main regret is that I never released the ball. I am sure that had it been delivered it would have been the equivalent of cricket's Lost Chord, a mighty delivery of speed and power never equalled before or since. As it was,

*The effect was spoiled*

all that happened was that I was carried from the field, moaning feebly and with the ball still clutched in my hand.

As the skipper said later: "When I saw you run into those stumps, I thought 'There goes the last of the Greens'."

In general, outdoor sport is better enjoyed with the aid of a little drink rather than a lot.

This is particularly true of such pursuits as rambling, fell-walking or climbing, where on a cold day there is the temptation to have a nip of Scotch to warm up right at the start of the day. A nip. Or two. Or three. For the first hour there is frenzied activity, people hurling themselves up 500 ft crags or rambling ten miles in the first hour. And then quite suddenly the whole thing falls apart. People are found asleep under boulders or behind trees. It is decided to advance the lunch-break, a halt is called at a pub, and that is the end of the ramble. The happy walkers are turned out of the pub at closing-time to sleep it off while waiting for the bus. Mind you, I don't complain if a day's walking finishes like that. But be clear in your own mind which way you want it to go before handing round the bottle.

The best way of ensuring that everyone keeps together on a Coarse ramble is for the leader to hand out a small drop of Scotch at the start, and then to keep in front of the party with the bottle. It is quite astonishing the mental spur that this has in curbing stragglers. It is, in fact, an old military trick. In India 150 years ago, conditions were so bad on the march that they used to carry the rum ration on a mule at the head of the column to make the men keep up.

Through unwise use of liquor while rambling, Uncle Walter nearly spent his honeymoon at his own funeral. He and my Aunt Gladys had gone walking on Dartmoor for their honeymoon, and were one day trapped by a sudden hailstorm. Walter's answer, as the weather got worse, was to apply himself more and more assiduously to his enormous flask of Scotch. After an hour he announced that he no longer felt any cold and he couldn't understand what Gladys was complaining about. After two hours he said he felt beautifully warm and drowsy and would just sit down for a little snooze, and plonked himself down by a crag, while the hail descended in torrents.

There weren't many vehicles across Dartmoor in those days, but Aunt Gladys managed to stop a lorry carrying coal, and Walter was conveyed back to the hotel in a stupor. Not that my aunt has ever received any thanks.

"I was as warm as toast, my boy," said Uncle Walter. "And if I had been insured I do not think your Aunt would have taken so much trouble."

Golf has the distinction of being one of the few outdoor sports where there are facilities for drinking while actually playing a game. Hockey players may sneak a quick snort at half-time; cricketers might hop into the pavilion between wickets. But in golf, not only can the player carry his own stuff about with him but some clubs provide bars halfway round the course, such as the little wooden tavern at Sunningdale.

This merely confirms my theory that golf is not a game at all, but a gift. If you have the gift, alcohol will not impair it. If you haven't the gift, you won't be any worse with alcohol, although you may well be considerably better.

Most golf clubs seem to have a friendly attitude to drink, and course and clubhouse focus round the bar. The odd thing though, is that they are obsessed with dress. I have been into a golf club and seen a member positively foaming with alcohol and nobody turned a hair. Yet some perfectly sober visitor coming in without a tie was ejected immediately, and insulted as well with a comment about "knowing how to behave decently in a public place." Meanwhile the drunk member in the corner was still foaming.

But then, golfers are people of peculiar emotions by normal standards. I have been in a golf club bar when a ball came flying through the window and the secretary merely commented, "I see Capt. Jones is having trouble with his grip again."

A golf club can be a Coarse Drinker's home-from-home, providing as it does facilities for eating, drinking, outdoor and indoor games, all in one place. All that has to be remembered is to wear the correct dress in the right room, and to address the secretary as "Major" unless told otherwise.

Sailing is a sport traditionally associated with drinking. Most people's idea of a sailing trip is that the crew lurch out of the yacht club completely plastered, weave back to the boat, set sail, and spend the entire trip knocking back great tumblerfuls of rum or whisky.

The reality is rather different. While it is true that the crew may well lurch out of the pub in jovial mood, if they do they are likely to be seasick and totally uninterested in drink during the voyage. In fact yachtsmen don't drink as much during a passage as is popularly supposed. To tell the truth, many skippers are terribly mean over the whole business. They hoard the boat's supplies of alcohol in a little locker and never offer any of it round.

If, after four hours on watch in an icy wind, you think to help yourself to a nip below, you can hear them whining from the cockpit, "I say old chap, do go easy on the brandy, we haven't got much, you know, and anyway I need you up here urgently."

However, one should not complain. Rather the mean skipper than the dreaded drunk one, or Tipsy Tyrant. They do not often get tight at sea; they have too much ashore, come aboard and insist on sailing whatever the weather. Thus the passage out of harbour is liable to be somewhat alarming, with much shouting and swerving and taking of the wrong channel. Typical is the man who actually sailed out of the East entrance to Cherbourg and sailed back in through the West, and would probably have gone round in circles for ever if the crew hadn't mutinied and headed the boat for England.

Mercifully, the horror of the Cock-Eyed Captain doesn't last long. By the time he's scraped his way out of harbour he's become sullen and morose, and with the first big sea he often turns a funny colour and goes below.

The danger comes if he doesn't. In that case he will certainly become prey to strange compulsions, such as insisting on right of way over oil tankers. I was once in the crew of a man who succeeded in taking 31 hours to sail from Boulogne to Folkestone, a distance of 26 miles if memory serves correctly. Most of that time was taken up making absurd course corrections to avoid imaginary hazards, together with an attempt to find a ship's raft which existed only in the captain's mind, or more likely his liver. During the whole trip he succeeded in remaining utterly and completely blotto, topping himself up with brandy every so often.

Like all drunken skippers he became convinced that everyone was against him and treated every offer of advice as mutiny. When we sighted land he got out his newly-purchased direction-finder and sat below twiddling knobs and calling out directions to me on the tiller. All the time we were sailing straight into Dungeness lighthouse. I said to him, "Look, old man, I'm sorry to bother you but we are just about to hit Dungeness lighthouse," and he merely barked back, "Absolute nonsense. The machine cannot lie, steer as directed." When we were about five minutes from piling up on the beach he suddenly bellowed, "Damn and blast it, I've been tuned in to Rye Airport by mistake. Do something for God's sake."

Later, of course, came the other syndrome of the Cock-Eyed Captain, a refusal to admit he had been wrong. "I don't want to appear critical, old fellow," he said in the pub that evening, "but you really mustn't let your attention wander when you're steering. You nearly had us on the beach off Dungeness this afternoon."

As a general rule for the Coarse Drinker, sailing is a disappointing sport. Tide and wind do not follow licensing hours and by the time you've made port, found a mooring, taken down sail, cooked a meal and rowed ashore, the crew are liable to be too tired for much jollity. Yacht clubs can be very gay places on Saturday nights, but the most gaiety comes from those who've been sensible enought to stay ashore all day.

Rugby is another sport traditionally associated with drink, and perhaps with more justification than sailing. The trouble is that rugby players are expected to conform to the legend that they are all beer-swilling extroverts. This can become a burden. Hearing that one is associated with rugby, people are liable to offer beer instead of gin-and-tonic and start trying to be back-slapping and jovial, because they think you're bound to behave that way.

I was at one party where the host treated me as if I was a sort of freak. I'd just come from a performance of Brecht's Edward IV and was looking for someone to discuss it with, and this idiot kept thrusting tankards into my hand and calling on me for a dirty song. To make things worse, so often one feels obliged to conform, with the result that both host and guest are acting out completely false roles. I asked what made him think I wanted to sing Eskimo Nell after going to the National Theatre, and he simply said, "But I thought you rugger men were all the same."

Having said that, it must be agreed that, thank heavens, beer is still an integral part of the game. A Coarse Drinker should be at home in a rugby club, although he may have to seek his level below the first team, where sometimes the result is considered more important than the beer. This, fortunately, is not always true of the other sides.

One of my greatest sporting regrets is that when I played I was not even fit enough to be one of those unsporting types who sneak a quick drink at half-time. I was always sick at the interval through sheer unfitness, exhaustion and cowardice and was much too ill to drink. There were about four of us in the side, all in the same state, and we used to lie together in a puddle gasping and retching while the

*Some of the team toughies were taking long pulls from rum bottles or even smoking cigarettes*

team toughies were taking long pulls from rum bottles or even smoking cigarettes.

The most dedicated Coarse Drinker I ever met was a rugby player. In those days we always travelled by coach and on the outward journey he would hand the driver a map with various places marked for a halt on the way back. He was also something of a practical joker and had a habit of telling customers at country pubs that he represented a famous firm of sports goods manufacturers. He claimed that a sealed number was deposited behind the bar, and whoever scored it on the dartboard would be presented with a set of golden darts.

Of course there was a mad rush to play darts, and after every throw he would be asked "Was that the sealed

number?" and would reply "No, but you're getting near."
Just before the coach left he'd cry "That's it. You've got
the sealed number. Collect the darts from the landlord,"
and vanish hastily, leaving behind a near-riot as customers
demanded the golden darts.

Later he bought a car and started going ahead of the coach
to spy out the alcoholic scene. This led to his undoing. He
arranged with the coach driver to stop at a certain pub and
went ahead to order a round of 25 drinks which cost something like £5. He came outside to greet us only to see the
coach disappear at sixty miles an hour, the driver having
mistaken the directions.

A Coarse Drinker who aspires to rugby should not fail
to visit some of those London pubs which act as clearing
houses for occasional Sunday sides, places where a man who
brings his kit along on Sunday lunchtime can have a choice
of a game with six or seven teams. Sometimes this leads to
odd situations. Many of the teams are from factories and
offices, and I shall never forget the sight of a hulking sixteen-
stone forward calling out "Shove, Exquisite Knitwear!"
while his opposite number was gasping, "For heaven's
sake tackle, Chic Deodorants!"

# 9

## On Overdoing it

*Beer is Best—Left Alone.*
1937 temperance advert

Every Coarse Drinker will at some time or another drink too much, although this does not mean that he will be drunk. Not that there is necessarily anything wrong in getting blotto occasionally. It releases emotional tensions and may even have the beneficial effect of making one give up drink for a few days.

The fault of getting tight lies in doing it in public. I firmly believe that as a man has more to drink he should be further and further removed from society. Most drunks are boring at the best and unpleasant at the worst. Ideally, a person who is going to have a bender should start off by shutting himself in a soundproof room and then get merrily tight, if necessary with a few like-minded friends.

Unfortunately, as we all know, people don't do this. They lurch all over public-bars, or weave down motorways with disastrous results.

Incidentally, it's interesting how people's attitude to drunkenness varies with the social status of the drunk. I was at a dinner at the Press Club, London, where the Sports Editor of a popular tabloid had to be helped up the stairs owing to an excess of whisky. A visitor asked who it was, and on being told he was sports editor of a popular newspaper commented, "Well, what do you expect?" Three hours later a representative of *The Observer* suddenly became completely rigid, stood swaying for a moment, and then slid slowly to the floor. The same visitor merely commented, "I see that reporter from *The Observer* is having a merry evening." That, however, is by the way.

One of the peculiarities of getting sozzled is that the drunk can tell when anybody else has had too much, but is totally incapable of applying the same judgement to himself. So here are a few tests which a Coarse Drinker can apply to discover whether he is on the way to having too much:

1. Does every woman in the room look terribly attractive, except your own wife?

2. Do you suddenly feel handsome, strong and good-looking?

3. Alternatively, do you suddenly feel bleary, bald and blotchy?

4. Do you wish to participate in some feat of physical danger or daring?

5. Do you suddenly love everyone?

6. Do you suddenly hate everyone?

7. Do you feel that you, and you alone, have discovered the secret of existence, hitherto denied to the human race?

8. Do you feel that life is just wonderful (or alternatively, hideous)?

9. Do you feel you could drink all night?

10. Do you feel incredibly witty?

It is now time to stop. Unfortunately, having reached that stage it is probably too late to stop anyway, and the following tests of drunkenness will have to be employed. Note that they are written in the third person, as the patient himself will be totally unable to apply them reliably.

1. Is the patient past caring what he drinks as long as it's alcoholic? (In this connection beware of a desire to drink hair-cream or some such nauseous mixture, simply because it is rumoured to contain wood alcohol.)

2. Does the patient feel the room is going round? (Note that the patient may well feel that the room is stationary and he is going round.)

3. Has the patient offered to marry/seduce/live with/ divorce anyone?

4. When the patient approaches a group of people do they move away?

5. If they don't move away does he blunder into them?

6. Does the patient keep complaining that the floor is unstable?

7. Has he lit the wrong end of a cigarette?

If the answer if Yes to the above, the patient should be locked up, except that by then he will be convinced he is perfectly sober and in any case there probably won't be anyone fit to lock him up.

Of course, it is impossible to generalise on how drink will take people, although I will go so far as to say that a man with one pint of good beer inside him is the nicest person on earth, genial, jovial, generous, courteous and of unerring judgement. Like myself.

There is, however, no telling what the same man will be like with six pints inside him. He may insist on lending you money; or equally strongly insist you owe him some. He may swear you are his oldest friend or his biggest enemy.

I have one friend who becomes incredibly benign when he has had too much. He actually used to leave the premises and wander about the road looking for people to help. It was rather embarrassing if he had a few drinks at lunch-time because we couldn't get him back to the office—he kept helping old ladies across Piccadilly Circus and giving money to match-sellers.

A problem concerned with celebrating is that of entering the house unobserved and unheard late at night, if one should be blessed with anxious parents or wife. .

One difficulty is that while the Coarse Drinker is under the impression that he is behaving in utter silence, stealthily tiptoeing about the premises, to the sober listener the whole performance sounds like a herd of elephants dancing the can-can.

It is at this critical moment that judgement goes completely astray and one may do something dreadful such as break an antique vase under the impression that you are knocking your pipe out on an ashtray.

And worse may happen. A chap who used to play cricket with me swears that after the club annual dinner, he tip-toed carefully into the house and climbed into bed with his sister-in-law, who was there on a visit. He had forgotten he was supposed to be sleeping in the spare room.

My friend Askew always takes the precaution, before a night out, of asking his wife to leave the lights in the house to form a sort of airport runway leading to the downstairs lavatory (Askew's inevitable first port of call in any house, whether he be drunk or sober).

One evening, however, the pattern of lights was disturbed by Askew's daughter, who went to bed late. Askew automatically guided himself by his principal approach-beacon (a low-wattage bulb two paces before the passage divided), entered what he believed was the appropriate room, and performed his task in what was later discovered to be the radiogram.

"Well, it had a lid just like a toilet," said Askew feebly next morning, under stern cross-examination from the entire family.

"You spoiled my record of Mick Jagger," complained his teenage daughter, bitterly. "How can I play it after what you did on it?"

"My dear," replied Askew with dignity, "for many years I have wanted to do that on Mick Jagger and I am glad that at last I have had the opportunity."

There are times when Askew doesn't get on too well with his daughter.

In applying these tests remember that a drunk has a habit of projecting his own deficiencies on to you.

As a friend always says at parties, "You must be drunk, you're looking blurred."

The result of over-indulgence is usually a hangover. The hangover is living testimony to the fallacy that alcohol physically does you good. Despite the obvious proof to the contrary my Uncle Walter still maintains that it does. He points to his brother-in-law as proof, although in reality his brother-in-law looks like what happens if you don't eat your cornflakes. I might have phrased that better but you know what I mean.

Never feel envious of people who do not have hangovers. They are Nature's protection-device, a way of trying to ensure you don't repeat the performance two days running. A useful test for deciding whether a person has had too much the night before, is whether he has difficulty in unscrewing the cap of his fountain pen.

One of the worst aspects of a hangover is that although it is clinically a symptom of poisoning, the sufferer will never receive the slightest sympathy. So it is no use a Coarse Drinker asking for it.

This seems rather unfair to me. It is true the injury has been self-inflicted in doing something that is basically

*On overdoing it*

frowned on by society. But that is true of a great many
injuries experienced by people enjoying themselves. It
always seems unjust that if a person indulges in the anti-
social sport of horse-racing, with all the gambling and
cheating that is involved, and falls off the horse and breaks
his skull, everyone is sorry for him. But if a person wakes
up after a heavy drinking session to find his face has turned
green; his mouth tastes as if a bird had nested there all
night; his head feels as if a gnome with a tiny pick was
digging a trench across the forehead; his stomach appears to
be full of hydrogen; a depression weighs down his spirits;
in other words, to discover he has a hangover, he will
receive far less sympathy than someone with a mere sprained
ankle playing football. In fact he will receive outright
condemnation, in terms such as, "It's your own fault, I've
told you not to drink so much."

Neither is the real hangover the affair of a moment. It
may well last all day (although Uncle Walter claims his
brother's hangover following his wedding has lasted all his
life). I can well recall celebrating the publication of a book
too well and still feeling dazed when interviewed on television the following evening. It was a terrible experience.
I couldn't even remember the name of the book I'd just
written and when they asked me what I thought was my
best book I named one by another author. At one point I
even forgot my own name.

Eventually the interviewer brought things to a conclusion
by trying to make light of it all ("Well, that just goes to
show that it's not only professors who're absent-minded").
Unfortunately, I was sitting behind him, numb with fatigue
and hangover, and a cigarette burning in my fingers suddenly
reached the skin, so the programme ended with a fiendish
howl. People rang up to ask who'd been killed.

The effect of the dreaded hangover on history is probably
vastly under-estimated. How many wars have been started
or stopped, how many battles lost and won through them?

The only evidence I can state with certainty is that the
British Army in the 18th Century abolished the practice of
saluting when the whites of an officer's eyes were visible.

8

This was because after the many regimental feast days, officers frequently had no whites to their eyes.

An old Coarse Drinking friend of mine, Geoffrey Webb, of Ealing, frequently tells how he was expelled from Penn State University, U.S.A., through a hangover.

He was taking a research degree there on an athletics scholarship. An athletics scholarship in the U.S. means just that—if the athletics cease so does the scholarship. Geoffrey had managed to keep in training but the night before the major meeting of the term he over-indulged at some student celebration.

Next day, when time came for the three-mile race, he found he was exhausted by the effort of walking to the start and on kneeling down to adjust his laces, he actually fell asleep. The coach, a stern New England puritan, said, "Good luck Geoffrey. Penn State is depending on you."

With what he considered fiendish cunning, Geoff staggered into the lead for the first three hundred yards and then suddenly collapsed on the track, groaning and clutching his ankle. The coach rushed to his aid, and all might have been well but for a terrible stench of beer that came out of the runner's sweating body.

The coach took one sniff and said sadly, "I would never have believed it of a member of Penn State athletic team. Geoffrey, your scholarship is terminated."

What really annoyed the coach was that my friend replied, "Aw gee, thanks coach." And he meant it. After six months without cigarettes, women or beer he'd had enough of competitive athletics.

Perhaps there is no aspect of drinking about which more fallacies are propounded than hangover cures. It is a subject which gives a field-day to fantasists.

A mystery about these alleged hangover cures, is that they almost always involve eating or drinking something nauseous. I simply can't understand why someone who's feeling ill should be expected to feel better after drinking a vile potion that would make him sick even in perfect health.

Typical of this sort of hangover myth is the Prairie Oyster, an alleged traditional hangover cure, consisting of a raw egg beaten up with Worcester sauce. It is one of those things everyone talks about without ever having experienced. And no wonder. Can you imagine drinking a raw egg and Worcester sauce on a hungover stomach?

The Prairie Oyster is much talked of by boasters and fantasists because it makes them sound men-of-the-world. Personally, I don't believe anybody has ever taken one without being sick.

I mention it simply because it is typical of a whole host of mythical hangover cures. In order that the Coarse Drinker will know which to avoid I will categorise them:

### The Hangover Cure Medical

This is usually propounded by a medical student: "After a thick night, old chap, I always go to the laboratory and take three and a half grains of Pheno-sodium-di-sulphide. It neutralises the phagosytes, you know." NOTE: Beware of nurses, who are also full of similar alleged and deadly cures, ranging from a whiff of nitrogen to strange black pills. I shall not forget the night sister at a London teaching hospital who having spent about five pounds of my money in helping me get a hangover, kindly gave me a "cure" next day which turned out to be a pill they gave drug addicts. I was prostrated for three days.

### The Hangover Cure Pharmaceutical

This is subtly different from the medical version and is dished out by chemists. It is always a brown liquid of particularly repulsive aspect, and it is typical of chemists that they can't resist putting in something to affect the bowels. So if driven to asking a chemist for a hangover cure, a Coarse Drinker should always stipulate whether he wishes a binding hangover cure or a laxative type. Distress and embarrassment may be caused by the wrong mixture, as I know to my cost.

### The Hangover Cure Bucolic

"Ah, me old beauty, if you'm been drinking too much of that there rough cyder, then first thing you'm must do on

*The Hangover Cure Bucolic*

wakin' up is to go down into the field and eat a piece of grass with dew on it from a field where the cows are grazing. Make sure 'e be fresh mind, or it won't work."

### The Hangover Cure Nauseous

Like the bucolic cure this involves taking something unpleasant, but without the country rite of prancing through the fields at dawn.

"What you want to do old chap, is to take a piece of raw liver, a portion of cold tripe, some cold fat and two teaspoonfuls of strawberry jam, mix them all together and swallow it in one gulp." NOTE: I don't consider the above any more ridiculous than a Prairie Oyster, and probably just as effective.

### The Hangover Cure Alcoholic

"I tell you whash old man, the only cure for a hangover ish a bottle of brandy. Neat. Ish wunnerful whash it doesh first thing in the mornin' . . ."

### The Hangover Cure Absurd

"You may find this a little odd, but honestly I always find

that it helps tremendously after a rough night to eat a small
piece of string with a knot in it . . ."

### The Hangover Cure Colonial

"When I was in the East, we found that the only thing that
would do a hangover any good was the juice of a coconut
picked from the top branch of a tall tree. Apparently the
ones on the lower branches aren't any good. We used to
have a glass of coconut juice and then stand on our heads for
five minutes. That's a tip I got from an old yoga-wallah
out there. Do that every morning and you'll never have a
hangover again. You'd often go into the club of a morning
after some big party and find five or six people standing on
their heads against the bar."

### The Hangover Cure Puritanical

"If a chap has been stupid enough to drink too much and
collect a hangover then the only cure is to take a cold bath
and run forty times round the local park . . ."

There is a minor branch of the Hangover Cure industry
which gives equally fatuous advice on how to avoid drinking
too much by taking something beforehand.

My landlady once made me eat a piece of raw kipper
before going out to a party because she said it would stop
me getting drunk. The only effect it had was to make me
violently ill. Other suggestions are to drink a pint of milk
or eat an orange before leaving. An old Cockney insisted to
me that a cold faggot, eaten uncooked, was the finest
sovereign remedy against a hangover. I think he was
probably right as the only effect following his advice must
have been to make the would-be drinker so ill that he'd
never get out of the house. That, in fact, seems a common
denominator to most of these tips and as with hangover
cures, I would advise the Coarse Drinker to stick only to
what has been tried and tested by himself.

My own hangover cure is simply cold water, bicarbonate
of soda, tea and aspirin in that order. But that doesn't

mean it would help anybody else. The golden wheeze is this:
A hangover cure is that which cures *your* hangover.

So if eating a piece of fried dung makes you feel better go ahead (subject to what I said in the foreword of this book). But please, let us have a rest from these fantasy cures.

Footnote: Uncle Walter has just come in and said, "My boy, why don't you tell them about the time your aunt made me take a stiff dose of bicarb before Harry's wedding to stop me getting tight?" I have no intention of going into details, but will merely state that the groom's "I do" in church was drowned by the loudest, most rasping belch I have ever heard in my life. The vicar told me afterwards he was convinced that the organ had broken down again. "We must get the lower register attended to," he said. "It keeps going off on its own accord."

# 10

# The Bad Pub Guide

*by MAL-DE-MER*

'Yet a gentleman may not keep a public-house: may he?' said I 'Not on any account' returned Herbert; 'but a public-house may keep a gentleman.'

CHARLES DICKENS (Great Expectations)

Who is Mal-de-Mer? Nobody knows. It is the pseudonym of a food and drink gourmet, a ruthless man with a hawklike stomach who has made himself famous with his reporting on places to drink and eat. No one knows where he will strike next. But one thing is certain. Mal-de-Mer is completely unbribable. Nothing, except money and a free meal, can make him alter his opinions.

*The Frogworthy Arms*

## The Frogworthy Arms, Cookenhead-on-Thames

I always feel that there is nothing to beat the atmosphere of a real old English country inn and here is one that is a tasteful blend of old and new. Major L. Rottingley-Watch-strap, who recently bought this delightful old place on the banks of the peaceful Thames, is justly proud of the many improvements he has made.

It used to be a ramshackle, half-timbered old building surrounded by desolate fields and only visited by a few locals. Now the hideous fields of buttercups and daisies have been replaced by the largest car park in Berkshire (with its own filling-station) while the mediaeval building with its sagging roof and rambling corridors has been torn down and rebuilt exactly like a mediaeval building with sagging roof and rambling corridors.

"We've even reproduced the old grandfather clock, in plastic," the merry Major told me. "Right down to the tick. We've got a tape recorder inside. You'd be amazed at the number of people who think it's the real thing."

But the Major has kept faith with tradition and at least three bricks from the old building have been incorporated in the new structure. One of them is over the massive open fireplace in the lounge (a replica of the old fireplace which was removed by the builders). A plaque says, "This brick could well be 500 years old, and was probably a brick that was here when Charles I fled past the inn during the Civil War. Undoubtedly the King's horses would have wanted watering during such a hard chase and what is more likely than that he would have stopped at the welcoming sign of the Frogworthy Arms to lead his horses to the gentle river's edge and enjoy himself with a stoup of the splendid liquor for which even then this ancient hostelry was renowned?"

How ancient and modern blend! Underneath is a notice:

ANY CARS LEFT IN THE CAR PARK
AFTER 11.15 P.M. WILL BE LOCKED IN
AND DISPOSED OF

A reminder that modern travellers like to refresh themselves (and their mechanical steeds!) at the Frogworthy.

The Frogworthy is, of course, noted for its food and we began our meal with a generous schooner of sherry in the lounge. But was it really necessary to lower the ceiling so much during the alterations? We were forced to drink in a kneeling position. But despite the realistic price of the sherry (£1·50 the glass) our tensions soon vanished in the olde-worlde atmosphere.

Then to the dining-room which overlooks the new car park. We chose tomato soup (95p) and Avocado pear (£2·58). I distinctly tasted tomato in my soup although my companion found the Avocado a trifle hard and bent her spoon on it. To follow we both had *le Biftek Frite a la mode de la maison* (steak) at £7·64 and my companion also had *les pommes de terre frites a l'huile* (chips) at 90p extra. Had we required them, tinned peas were available at 75p per portion. Bread was free, but unobtainable.

The meal was washed down with a modest Beaujolais at £9·35 the bottle. A small complaint about the drinks service. Was it essential to charge 50p for a glass of water? It is often served free, even in the West End. Ice was available at 25p a cube.

Only one incident marred a delightful meal. After paying the bill (£35·85 for the two of us), together with the 25 per cent service charge, we were rather surprised when the waiter demanded a tip as well. I handed him a five pound note but he spat upon it and struck me over the head with a large silver tray. But our cheerful Major assured us that if it happened again, the man would be spoken to severely.

## The Marquis of Grimthorpe, Battersea, S.W.11

This is one of those grand old Victorian London public-houses of which foreigners are so envious, and it stands on a busy corner in South London. A notice behind the bar announces, "Your genial hosts are Ron and Maureen Bloggs" and both of them do their best to make customers welcome,

*The Marquis of Grimthorpe, Battersea*

although they are so busy they may not be able to give them the personal attention they would wish. .

After all, the Marquis of Grimthorpe (known locally, with typical London wit, as The Charnel House) has seventeen bars. Food is served in three of them, music in five, and beer in most of them (even the landlord has not visited them all, so he is a little uncertain of these figures).

The range of beers is fantastic and Ron and Maureen are justly proud of what can be served. Customers have a choice of bitter, mild, best bitter, worst bitter, special bitter and the brewery's new line—Blastoff. This is a new beer specially-designed for young drinkers, being completely tasteless, largely non-alcoholic and costing 10p a pint.

Snacks are available everywhere in the pub and substantial lunches in the Eatery (formerly the dining-room).

The food side is presided over by the genial chef, a burly Cockney character known locally as Shiner Bartlett. Shiner, a former night-club security officer, has his own unique method of cooking which although unconventional is highly successful.

"The secret of good pub-cooking is in the labelling," he said. You tell a public-bar customer he's eating steak pie and he'll believe yer. He's in too much of a hurry to notice whether that smear of gravy under the crust is chicken or steak. In any case, all my pies look the same and taste the same.

"It's my proud boast that my pies are completely interchangeable. As one who has studied this 'ere subject scientific-like I believe this is the era of the all-purpose pub-pie."

Shiner was bitter about what he called "prodnosed bureaucrats" who interfere with his artistic freedom as a chef.

"We had a geezer from the Town Hall here last week," he protested, "who started complaining about mouse-droppings in me sugar. Me! Who spends hours picking 'em out by hand. I've got a bucketful of mouse-droppings in that corner that I've picked out from the sugar single-handed. But there's no justice, mate."

I would have liked to have lingered longer in the Marquis of Grimthorpe but although it was only ten past two Ron and Maureen were plainly anxious for a well-earned rest. Bells clanged, lights flickered, and three Alsatian dogs appeared snarling behind the bar, while all round resounded the time-honoured cry of "Time ladies and gentlemen, please! Your glasses please!"

The last plea was somewhat unnecessary, as on the stroke of the first bell Shiner Bartlett's brother comes round the tables seizing all glasses and bottles whether empty or full, sometimes in mid-air on the way to a customer's lips.

But as our jovial landlord said, as he jostled me out of the door, "You have to be firm in a big place like this. Believe me, your good old South London working-class bloke only appreciates you if you're firm. But they're a great lot really."

## The Easy Bird Disco-Tavern, Boreville New Town

The Easy Bird is one of the newest pubs in the country, designed to serve a population of 100,000 in this area of Boreville New Town. I say pub, but the Easy Bird represents the supersonic age of drinking, and the brewers prefer to call it "an alcoholically-orientated entertainment complex."

*The Easy Bird Disco-Tavern*

"The idea is to get right away from the old hideous darts and half-of-bitter image of a pub," said a brewery spokesman, and they certainly have.

The centre of the Easy Bird is the teenage bar, which covers the entire ground floor of three acres. Here young people can telephone their record requests to a live disc jockey sitting behind a bullet-proof screen at one end of the room.

The range of drinks has been designed to satisfy the young palate as well. A bar fifty feet long serves draught coco-cola and brown ale.

At the back of the complex is a special children's bar with a heated porch into the garden, where mothers and fathers can sit quaffing their drinks while their children gurgle contentedly in their prams. If nipper is hungry, a mother can go into a special room to feed her child, taking her drink with her. Meanwhile, the hard-working breadwinner of the family might like to try his luck on one of the three hundred fruit machines installed round the walls.

It was impossible to ask customers or staff of the Easy Bird for their opinions as, owing to the volume of noise from the pop music, all conversation is conducted in signs. The manager does not serve behind the bar, but works from a central office. However he told me by telephone that the place is flourishing.

"We don't stand still here," he shouted. "You won't find a dartboard or a bar-billiard table in here, nor a customer under 25. We're thinking of giving up selling beer soon—that's the next logical step.

"Don't forget we were the first pub in the country to have a live D.J. Come to think of it, we were also the first pub to have a dead D.J., but don't print that. The kids didn't mean no harm."

The current manager is the third in the Easy Bird's brief life of two months. The first went blind through looking at the psychedelic lighting, and the second is in hospital with a punctured eardrum. But as the present manager put it, "They were just casualties on the road to progress."

## The King Charles III Inn and Steak Bar

This is a superb example of the way in which many dull old pubs are being transformed into swinging steak-houses to cater for the growing habit of eating out. There are no fewer than thirteen different restaurants in the King Charles III, each with a different menu. Examples are: The Winking Cavalier: Steak, duck, scampi; The Randy Roundhead: Scampi, duck, steak; The Jovial Ironside: Duck, steak, scampi. Similarly varied selections are available elsewhere.

My half of roast duck was perhaps a little erratically cooked, being burned on the outside and still frozen in the middle, but this was compensated for by the friendly service from a waitress who engagingly addressed me as "luv", and who insisted on tasting one of my chips to see if they were all right.

Food is cooked on an open grill in front of your eyes, so a customer can see his own choice being prepared, although unfortunately a dense cloud of blue smoke and spitting fat prevented my seeing this.

My one complaint would be that the chef appeared a trifle young, being about sixteen, and with a distressing habit of wiping plates with his waist-length hair. But I am assured that he is fully-experienced. Indeed, he has had five jobs in the last three months.

# Postscript: Uncle Walter's Piece

I'm glad of the opportunity to contribute to this book as I've a lot of useful knowledge gathered in a lifetime's boozing which I'd like to pass on to you younger fellows. So here goes:

If you are troubled with corns, you want to try rubbing a little gin on them. They'll soon vanish. You can try it with warts too.

A good tip for getting rid of blackheads is to bathe them in gin and bitter lemon.

If you wake up feeling out of sorts put some gin in your morning tea.

If your wife is bad-tempered give her some gin.

Gin is a good cure for constipation.

I always find that gin is a good cure for diarrhoea as well.

If you don't want your wife to know you are drinking spirits, order a half of bitter for yourself at the bar, and slip a gin in it.

You will never have hair growing out of your ears if you drink a half a bottle of gin every day. I know this from personal experience.

*(There are 500 more pages in the same vein, but there is only space for this brief extract.)*

*Uncle Walter's Piece*

If you would like a complete list of Arrow books
please send a postcard to
P.O. Box 29, Douglas, Isle of Man, Great Britain.